Essential GCSE ICT for WJEC
Teacher's Resource Guide

Folens

United Kingdom: Folens Publishers, Waterslade House, Thame Rd, Haddenham, Buckinghamshire HP17 8NT.

www.folens.com

Ireland: Folens Publishers, Greenhills Road, Tallaght, Dublin 24.

Email: info@folens.ie

Editor:	Geoff Tuttle
Project development:	Adrian Moss (Instructional Design Ltd) with Rick Jackman (Jackman Publishing Solutions Ltd)
Design development:	Greengate Publishing Services
Layout artist:	The Manila Typesetting Co.
Illustrations:	The Manila Typesetting Co.
Software architecture and design:	Haremi Ltd
Cover design:	Jump To! www.jumpto.co.uk
Cover image:	Courtesy of Chris Harvey/ Fotolia.com

First published 2010 by Folens Limited

Every effort has been made to contact copyright holders of material used in this publication. If any copyright holder has been overlooked, we should be pleased to make any necessary arrangements.

British Library Cataloguing in Publication Data.
A catalogue record for this publication is available from the British Library.

ISBN 978-1-85008-542-3

Contents

Topic 23 Legal and ethical issues

Topic 24 Staying safe online

Topic 25 Data protection issues

Topic 26 Health issues

Topic 27 Emerging technologies

Acknowledgements

Using the CD-ROM

Home screen

The Home screen provides links to the main features of the program: the **Resource Finder** where you can search for and launch or save all of the resources available; the **Glossary** containing key words and their definitions; and detailed **Help** information.

You may return to the Home screen at any time by clicking .

Resource Finder

To open the Resource Finder click 🔍 on the Home screen.

The Resource Finder allows you to access any of the resources on the CD-ROM. The table on this screen lists the titles of the resources, and displays a description of each resource, the topic to which the resource is linked and the resource's file format.

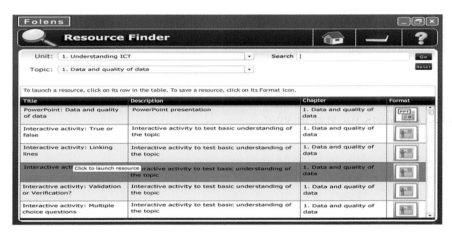

To list only those resources linked to a specific unit or topic, select from the drop-down lists at the top of the screen.

Searching for a resource

To search for a resource on a specific topic, type a word or short phrase in the Search box and click the **Go** button.

The search works in conjunction with the drop-down lists. The program will search the titles, descriptions and key words associated with resources in the unit and topic currently selected, and display the results of your search in the table on the screen.

To clear the current search and return to the full list of resources, click the **Reset** button at any time.

Launching resources

To launch a resource directly from the program, simply click on the row in which the resource appears in the table. Resources such as PDF files and PowerPoint presentations will launch in your computer's default application for that resource type.

Interactive activities will launch in a separate window. It is possible to launch more than one interactive activity at a time and navigate between them using the Windows Task bar.

Within an interactive activity you can click to open the on-screen toolbox.

The toolbox provides a freehand pen and highlighter for annotating the screen. The notes feature also allows you to type text onto note paper that can be dragged to any position on the screen.

You can print the current screen at any time by clicking .

Once you have completed an activity click the X button to close it. Your changes will not be saved.

Saving resources

To save a resource to your computer/network for you or your students to use later, click on the resource's icon in the Format column. In the Save resource window that appears, browse to the folder in which you wish to save the resource and click **OK**. A message will be displayed to confirm the resource has been successfully saved in your chosen location.

To launch a saved resource, simply open the file from the location in which you saved it. Some resources are made up of more than one file stored in a folder. To launch these resources, open the folder and double-click the 'start.exe' file.

Glossary

To open the Glossary, click  on the Home screen or Resource Finder screen.

To find a word or term, click on the first letter of the word/term (note, there are no words/terms beginning with the letters shown in grey). All words/terms beginning with the selected letter will be listed on the screen. To view the definition of a word/term, simply click on it.

Help

To view this help document, click ? on the Home screen or Resource Finder screen.

Introduction to the materials on the CD-ROM

If you are a teacher/lecturer, the teacher support material will give you all you need to teach the GCSE-Level in ICT effectively. The CD-ROM contains interactive and non-interactive digital materials, including answers to questions in the student book and lots of new questions.

Non-interactive materials

Answers: are given to the Questions and Case studies in the student book, with page cross-references for ease of use.

There are also additional features on the CD-ROM with answers supplied and these can be used for homework.

Activities

Activities are used to build up knowledge and skills without being in examination question format. There are many activities that involve students undertaking some research or organizing their ideas, thoughts and knowledge in a certain way by producing mind maps, presentations, etc. These activities are in addition to those contained in the student book.

Case studies and Case study questions

Questions are usually asked in a context and students need to know and understand how ICT can be used in different situations and how businesses and organizations use ICT. Case studies give students information as to how ICT can be used in a wide range of situations and this will give them practice answering questions that relate to a scenario and also enable them to answer questions on a concept where an example is expected.

You may choose to include some of these Case studies in mock examinations.

Multiple-choice questions: although multiple choice questions do not feature in the examination, they are a useful way for the students to assess their knowledge. Each question has four possible answers.

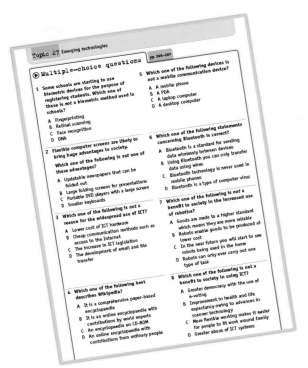

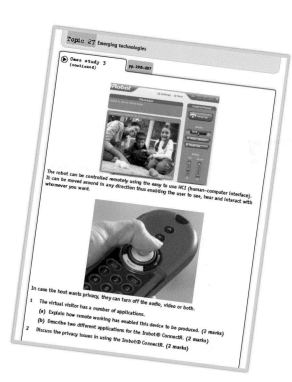

Worksheets

These are activities that students can complete on the sheet but you can also display them on the screen for them to answer thus avoiding the need to make copies.

Detailed answers to these worksheets are included.

Interactive materials

The wide range of interactive activities helps to reinforce students' knowledge of material in an engaging and motivating way. The interactive activities are suitable for whole-class teaching at an interactive whiteboard or for students to use independently at individual computers. As the CD-ROM also contains answers to the textbook questions, it is recommended that you save any activities you wish students to use independently to a shared location on your network.

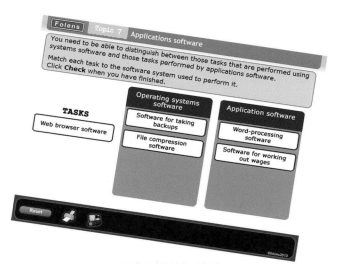

Drag and drop (matching): students drag descriptions to match them with the correct terms.

Fill in the gaps (drop-down lists): students complete some statements or a passage of text by selecting the correct missing words from the drop-down lists.

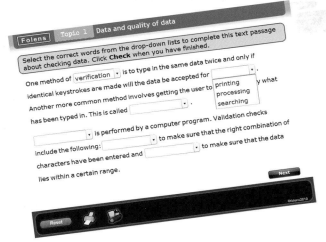

Linking lines: students match up items (either text or images) by connecting them with a line.

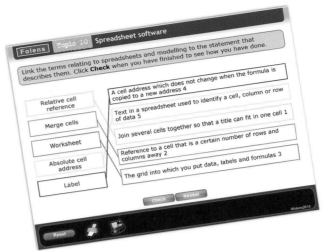

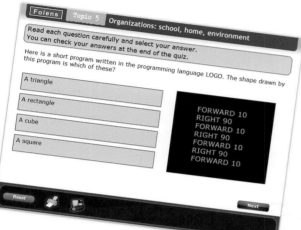

Multiple-choice questions: although multiple choice questions do not feature in the examination, they are a useful way for the students to assess their knowledge. Each question has four possible answers. Student answers are marked by the computer when all questions have been answered.

PowerPoint presentations: help explain topics and add further information to the material contained in the student book.

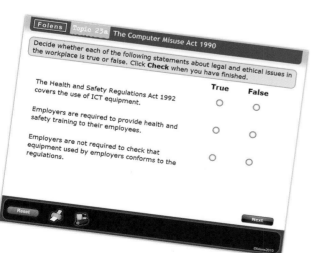

True or false: students are given a number of statements and they have to decide whether the statements are true or false. The computer marks their answers.

Launching the program

To run the program directly from the CD-ROM, insert the disc in your disc drive and select the 'Run from CD-ROM' option. If the disc does not auto run, browse the contents of the disc and click the 'start.exe' file. Some operating systems will require you to right-click on this file and select 'Run as administrator' for the program to function correctly.

If you have already installed the program to your standalone computer or network, double-click the 'Essential GCSE ICT for WJEC CD-ROM' desktop shortcut.

If the program has not already been activated, the activation screen will appear. You may use the program in trial mode for the number of days shown, or click the link on the screen to register online and obtain an activation code if you have purchased the program.

Installation instructions

Standalone computer

1. Insert the CD-ROM in your disc drive and select the 'Install' option. If the disc does not auto run, browse the contents of the disc and click the 'start.exe' file. Some operating systems will require you to right-click on this file and select 'Run as administrator' for the installer to function correctly.
2. The Installation wizard will appear. It is recommended that you close all other programs before installing the program. Once you have closed all other programs and are ready to continue click 'Next'.
3. Please read the licence agreement carefully. If you accept the terms of the licence click 'I agree' to proceed with installation. If you do not accept the terms click 'Cancel' to abort the installation.
4. To install to the default installation location shown click 'Install'. If you wish to install to a different location click 'Browse' and select an alternative location before clicking 'Install'.

5. It may take several minutes for all of the program files to be installed. When the installation is complete, you will be able to click 'Finish' to close the Installation wizard.

Network

1. To install to your network, install the program at your network server following steps 1–5 above. Ensure the program is installed to a shared location accessible by the appropriate users.
2. Create a shortcut for users to the 'start.exe' file located within the installed program folder.
3. If the program has not already been activated, the activation screen will appear when the program is launched. It is only necessary to register and activate the program once at the server or any workstation to prevent the activation screen from appearing.

VLE

If you have purchased the program, registered and activated it, a 'Download VLE pack' link on the Home screen will enable you to download the same resources available within the standalone program, in SCORM-compliant format for use within your VLE. Further details can be found in the vle readme text file that you can also download.

Uninstall instructions

To uninstall the program, click on the file called 'uninstall.exe' in the installed program folder. The uninstaller will permanently delete all files in the same folder as the 'uninstall.exe' file.

Minimum specification

Windows® 2000, XP, Vista, 7
Pentium III 500 MHz
256 MB RAM
2 GB hard disk space
800 x 600 screen resolution
Adobe Reader
Microsoft Office 2000
Microsoft® Internet Explorer® or Firefox®
(for VLE version only)

▶ Worksheet 1

Error checking

Here is a table containing the names of validation checks and what they are designed to check. The only problem is that they have been mixed up. Using the new table, write in the correct checks in the spaces.

Name of validation check	Description of what it is designed to check
Range check	A number placed at the end of a string of numbers to check that they have been correctly input into the computer.
Data type/character check	Checks to make sure that the data contains the correct combination of letters and numbers.
Presence check	To make sure that a number lies within a certain range.
Check digit	Making sure that the right type of data is entered. For example, numbers can only be entered into a numeric field.
Format check	Ensuring that data has been entered into a field.

Name of validation check	Description of what it is designed to check
Range check	
Data type/character check	
Presence check	
Check digit	
Format check	

▶ Worksheet 2   pp. 1–9

Data and quality of data anagrams

Here are some words or phrases that have been jumbled up. The words are connected with Data and quality of data. Can you work out what they are? There is a clue to help you.

1 Iron moan fit   *Hint: What data is turned into after processing.*

Answer: _____

2 Process gin   *Hint: Performing a calculation is an example of this.*

Answer: _____

3 Cast iron tan   *Hint: Example of a piece of business.*

Answer: _____

4 Lodge knew   *Hint: You get this when you apply rules to information.*

Answer: _____

5 Ding once   *Hint: Coding data on collection.*

Answer: _____

6 Violin data   *Hint: The computer checking data is correct.*

Answer: _____

7 Constant air   *Hint: A type of error made when transferring data.*

Answer: _____

8 Prison into sat   *Hint: The swapping around of characters.*

Answer: _____

9 Creep sen   *Hint: A check to make sure data has been filled in.*

Answer: _____

10 Shah   *Hint: A total that does not make sense.*

Answer: _____

Creating validation messages from validation expressions

The table below contains validation expressions used in a database created using Microsoft Access. Fill in the table by writing a suitable message that would appear should the user type in data that breaches the validation expression.

Validation expression	Message appearing if expression is *not* valid
>1 And <100	
>=1 And <=20	
>=0	
>30	
>#1/01/08#	
>=#5/04/08#	
Like"A?????"	
= 1 Or 2 Or 3	
>=#01/01/06# And <#31/12/06#	

▶ Worksheet 4   p. 4

What do these codes mean?

Data is often encoded. A good coding system is fairly obvious. Can you work out what each of the following coding systems are?

1   M/F

Meaning: _____

2   FD04RTF

Meaning: _____

3   S/M/L/XL/XXL

Meaning: _____

4   0151/0121/0161/0181

Meaning: _____

5   MAN/LHR

Meaning: _____

6   U, PG, 12, 15, 18

Meaning: _____

7   GBP, USD, EUR

Meaning: _____

8   Y7/Y8/Y9

Meaning: _____

9   .bmp/.jpg/.gif

Meaning: _____

10 A*/A/B/C/D/E

Meaning: _____

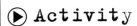

▶ **Activity** pp. 6–7

Spreadsheet cell validation checks

Here are some validation checks that are to be applied to a range of cells in a worksheet created using spreadsheet software.

For each of the checks, give the name of the validation check and also give a brief explanation of how the check will help prevent incorrect data being entered.

1 Validation check 1

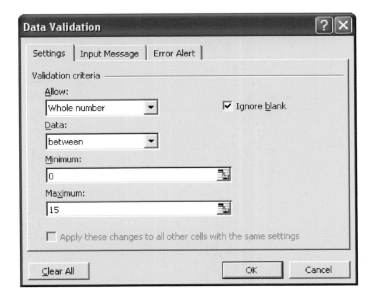

Name of validation check _____

Explanation

_____

_____

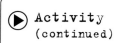

Activity (continued)   pp. 6–7

2   Validation check 2

Name of validation check _____

Explanation

_____

_____

3   Validation check 3

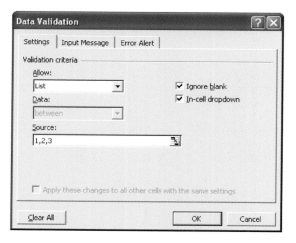

Name of validation check _____

Explanation

_____

_____

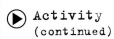

▶ **Activity** (continued)   pp. 6–7

4   Validation check 4

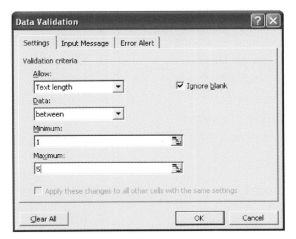

Name of validation check _____

Explanation _____

_____

_____

5   Validation check 5

Name of validation check _____

Explanation _____

_____

_____

▶ Multiple-choice questions

1 Which one of the following is *not* a reason for coding data?

   A Typing in coded data takes less time

   B Takes up less storage space (less important as storage media is cheap)

   C It is easier to check that a code is accurate using validation checks

   D Coding data makes it easier for humans to understand it

2 Data is which one of these?

   A What you get out of a computer

   B What you put into a computer

   C What the computer does with the data

   D A type of job

3 Raw facts and figures are referred to as which one of these?

   A Data

   B Validation

   C Knowledge

   D Information

4 Data that has been processed by the computer is called which one of these?

   A Data

   B Validation

   C Knowledge

   D Information

5 Here is a list of names: Stephen, Amy, Luke, Emily

They are put into alphabetical order: Amy, Emily, Luke, Stephen

This is an example of which one of the following?

   A Calculating

   B Processing

   C Knowledge

   D Validation

6 GIGO stands for which one of the following?

   A Garbage Input Garbage Output

   B Grand Input Grand Output

   C Nothing

   D Garbage In Garbage Out

7 Encoding means which one of these?

   A Breaking a secret code

   B Putting data into a code

   C Making a code secret

   D Processing data

8 Which one of the following is a disadvantage in using ICT?

   A You are reliant on the computer system

   B It is much faster to access data

   C The storage of data takes much less space

   D It is very easy to transfer data

9 The following is entered into an ICT system: GCSE, C, 50, 45

This represents which one of the following?

   A Data

   B Information

   C Validation

   D Output

10 Which one of these is *not* a measure of the quality of data?

   A Whether the data is fit for purpose

   B The accuracy of the data

   C Whether the data is unbiased

   D How much the information cost to produce

ANSWERS

Questions A

▶ **TEXTBOOK PAGE 3**

1 (a) Data (1)
   (b) Information (1)
   (c) Knowledge (1)
2 (a) One mark for answers such as:
        Accurate (1) – e.g., must give each student the same questions (1)
        Fit for purpose (1) – e.g., must be able to decide from the answers who is the best (1)
        Not biased (1) – no leading questions that point towards a preferred answer (1)
   (b) Biased (1) because the questioner is asking for agreement/asking a leading question (1)
3 (a) One mark for each type to a maximum of three marks.
        • Words
        • Numbers
        • Sound
        • Video
        • Images
   (b) One mark for each relevant point to a maximum of three marks. Example such as:
        Data such as 4, 6, 12, 9 are entered into a computer (1). These are the sales made by a salesperson of cars sold in a week. The data can be processed by calculating the average (1). The average number of cars sold in a month is the information. (1)

Questions B

▶ **TEXTBOOK PAGE 5**

1 Two marks for an explanation allocated as follows:
   Putting data into a code (1) which reduces the size of the data (1)
   One mark for an example such as:
   Airport code MAN = Manchester (1)
2 One mark for each reason to a maximum of two marks.
   • Coded data is quicker to type in
   • More data can appear on the screen
   • It takes up less storage space
   • It is easier to check a code using validation checks
   • It is faster to access data that is coded
   • It is quicker to send the data over a network
3 One mark each for two advantages such as:
   • Less storage space is needed
   • Data is easily copied – data can be copied very quickly
   • Easier to back up
   • Easily transferred
   • Fast access to stored data
   • Data can be put into a secret code when stored (i.e. encrypted)
   One mark each for two disadvantages such as:
   • Data can be copied quickly and easily unless protected
   • Reliance on networks
   • Training needed
   • Security problems

Questions C

▶ **TEXTBOOK PAGE 7**

1 (a) Three marks allocated as follows:
        An extra number added at the end of a long number (1), which is calculated from all the other numbers (1)

and is used to ensure that the number has been input correctly (1)
   (b) One mark for each example to a maximum of two marks such as:
        • ISBN (International Standard Book Number)
        • Bar code/article number on items in a supermarket
        • Bank account number
        • Utility (gas, electricity, water, phone) customer number
        • Part number
2 (a) One mark for this date is far into the future
   (b) One mark for the month contains the number 13, which is impossible
   (c) One mark for the 30 February is impossible
3 (a) One mark for an appropriate check and one mark for the reason.
        • Format check (1) – only allows the letters and numbers in the format chosen (1)
        • Length check (1) – checks that the code contains exactly 9 characters (1)
   (b) One mark for an appropriate check and one mark for the reason.
        • Range check (1) – to ensure the salary is within a certain range, e.g., greater than 0 but less than a certain salary (1)
        • Data type check (1) – to ensure that currency/number has been entered (1)
4 One mark for the example and one mark each to a maximum of two marks for each point.
   • A person is typing in an order from an order form (1)
   • The form says the quantity is 89 and the person mistakenly types 98 (1)
   • There is a range check which says you cannot enter less than zero or more than 100 (1)
   • The wrong number passes the range check so it is valid but it is still incorrect (1)

Questions D

▶ **TEXTBOOK PAGE 9**

1 One mark for each explanation (i.e. two marks total).
   Transcription errors – errors that occur when transferring data from a form (e.g., application form, order form, etc.) to a computer (1). Can be caused by mishearing what a person says over the telephone and entering it into the computer (1)
   Transposition errors – errors made when typing quickly and involves typing letters or numbers in the wrong order (1). For example a student number 1032 entered as 1023 (1).
2 (a) One mark for a definition and two marks max for two points relating to why some have them.
        • Checks that important data has been entered (1)
        • Checks that important fields have not been left blank (1)
        • Without this important information the order could not be fulfilled (1)
   (b) One mark for a field needing a presence check and one mark for a field that does not need one.
        Fields needing a presence check
        • Name (1)
        • Address (1)
        • Postcode (1)
        • Item number (1)

- Credit card number (1)
- Expiry data (1)

Fields *not* needing a presence check
- Telephone number
- Email address
- Work telephone number
- Date of birth (for marketing purposes)

Test yourself

▶ **TEXTBOOK PAGE 10**

A Data
B information
C GIGO
D Knowledge
E quality
F Processing
G code
H transcription
I transposition
J Validation
K Verification

Examination style questions

▶ **TEXTBOOK PAGE 11**

1 (a) One mark for explanation of the abbreviation:
Garbage In Garbage Out
One mark for further explanation such as:
If the data input is wrong then the information output will be wrong

(b) One mark for each point to a maximum of three marks such as:
- It could be life threatening – if the mistakes involved a patient in a hospital and they were given the wrong treatment.
- It could cost money – may have additional costs if customer is sent the wrong order.
- You could lose customers – if mistakes are made the customers may go elsewhere in future.
- You could be prosecuted – if mistakes were in personal data and the person was refused a job, a loan, etc., you could be fined.

2 One mark for each point to a maximum of two marks such as:
- Visual check/proof read (1) – check that what has been typed into the computer is identical to what is on the form (1)
- Double entry of data (1) – key the same details in twice (best to use different people) and only if both versions are the same will it be accepted for processing (1)

3 One mark for each mistake (they must be distinctly different) to a maximum of three marks.
- Spelling mistakes
- Typing the same data twice
- Leaving an important field blank
- Transposing letters and numbers
- Misreading a word or number from the document they are taking the data from

4 One mark for each point to a maximum of three marks.
- Format check so date is entered in the form dd/mm/yyyy
- Presence check to check that data has been entered

- Range check to check that the number of days does not go past that for the month
- Range check to check that a date of birth is not after today's date

5 (a) One mark for 21059810J

(b) One mark for each point to a maximum of two marks such as:
- A check performed by a computer program (1)
- To restrict the data being entered (1)
- So that it is allowable and reasonable (1)
- So that it obeys certain rules before it is accepted (1)

(c) One mark for each of two methods. Examples include:
Range check
- Check that the whole number lies between 1 and 99999999
- Check that the date part lies in the range for acceptable dates, e.g. not 31/02/10, which is impossible
- Check that the year of joining is not before the fitness club opened

Format check
- The first 8 characters are all numbers
- The ninth/last character must be a letter
- The ninth/last character must be either J or S
- There must be 9 characters in total

(d) (i) Because people can have the same date of birth and join the club in the same year (1)
(ii) Can get more than one person with the same membership number (1)
You can get confused between members (1)

6 (a) One mark for each point to a maximum of three marks.
- A check digit is a number placed at the end of the block of numbers (1).
- The computer performs a calculation using all the numbers to work out this extra number (1).
- If the check digit is the same as that calculated by the other numbers, it means that all the numbers have been entered correctly (1).

(b) One mark for each application to a maximum of two marks.
- Luggage labelling at an airport (1)
- Library tickets (1)
- International Standard Book Numbers (ISBNs)
- Loyalty cards (1)
- Utility bills (e.g., gas, electricity, water, telephone)

(c) (i) One mark for similar answer to: only allows a certain combination of letters, numbers and other symbols to be entered, e.g. a postcode L23 6TH
(ii) One mark for similar answer to: checks to ensure an important field such as name or address has details entered for an online order.
(iii) One mark for similar answer to: check to make sure that the data sent is the same as that received when data is transmitted from one computer to another.
(iv) One mark for similar answer to: ensures a number being entered is within a certain range of values, e.g. between 1 and 100.

Worksheet 1: Error checking

▶ TEACHER'S RESOURCE GUIDE TOPIC 1 PAGE 1

Name of validation check	Description of what it is designed to check
Range check	To make sure that a number lies within a certain range.
Data/character type check	Making sure that the right type of data is entered. For example, numbers can only be entered into a numeric field.
Presence check	Ensuring that data has been entered into a field.
Check digit	A number placed at the end of a string of numbers to check that they have been correctly input into the computer.
Format check	Checks to make sure that the data contains the correct combination of letters and numbers.

Worksheet 2: Data and quality of data anagrams

▶ TEACHER'S RESOURCE GUIDE TOPIC 1 PAGE 2

1 Information
2 Processing
3 Transaction
4 Knowledge
5 Encoding
6 Validation
7 Transaction
8 Transposition
9 Presence
10 Hash

Worksheet 3: Creating validation messages from validation expressions

▶ TEACHER'S RESOURCE GUIDE TOPIC 1 PAGE 3

Validation expression	Message appearing if expression is *not* valid
>1 And <100	The number entered must be over 1 and under 100. Note this does not include the numbers 1 or 100.
>=1 And <=20	The number entered must be between 1 and 20 including the numbers 1 and 20.
>=0	A zero or positive number must be entered.
>30	A number greater than 30 must be entered.
>#1/01/08#	A date after the date 1/01/08 must be entered.
>=#5/04/08#	A date on or after the date 05/04/08 must be entered.
Like"A?????"	The data entered must be six characters long starting with the letter A.
= 1 Or 2 Or 3	The data being entered must be 1, 2 or 3.
>=#01/01/06# And <#31/12/06#	The data being entered must be in the year 06.

Worksheet 4: What do these codes mean?

▶ **TEACHER'S RESOURCE GUIDE TOPIC 1 PAGE 4**

1 M/F
  Male or Female
2 FD04RTF
  A car registration – registered between 1 April 04 and 31 Aug 04
3 S/M/L/XL/XXL
  Sizes for clothes
4 0151/0121/0161/0181
  The area STD codes for land lines
5 MAN/LHR
  Airport codes for Manchester, London Heathrow
6 U, PG, 12, 15, 18
  Film classifications
7 GBP, USD, EUR
  Currencies Great Britain Pound, United States Dollar, Euro
8 Y7/Y8/Y9
  The three Key Stage 3 years in a school
9 .bmp/.jpg/.gif
  File extensions used for graphics files
10 A*/A/B/C/D/E
  The possible grades for GCSE

Activity: Spreadsheet cell validation checks

▶ **TEACHER'S RESOURCE GUIDE TOPIC 1 PAGE 5**

1 Name of validation check: Range check
  Explanation: Only allows the user to enter whole numbers between and including 0 and 15.
2 Name of validation check: Range check
  Explanation: Only allows the user to enter a whole number less than 10.
3 Name of validation check: Restricting the user to a list.
  Explanation: Only allows the user to choose a value of 1, 2 or 3 from a drop-down list.
4 Name of validation check: Format check
  Explanation: Only allows from one character to five characters inclusive to be entered.
5 Name of validation check: Range check
  Explanation: Allows any number above zero to be entered.

Multiple-choice questions

▶ **TEACHER'S RESOURCE GUIDE TOPIC 1 PAGE 8**

1D, 2B, 3A, 4D, 5B, 6D, 7B, 8A, 9A, 10D

▶ Worksheet 1   pp. 21–23

The Internet: What do these terms mean?

Here is a list of terms in alphabetical order. Put the meanings next to the term. If you don't know what the meaning is, then use one of the glossaries available on the Internet.

Term	Meaning
Browser	
Chat room	
Cookie	
Download	
Email	
FAQ	
Hacker	
HTML	
ISP	
Link	
Modem	
Surfing	
User-ID	
Webpage	

The future of mobile phones

The latest mobile phones are full of features. Later on in the course you will be looking at emerging technologies. These are technologies that are likely to change the future.

For this activity you have to think about the future of mobile phones and what you would like them to do that they do not currently do. Write down a list here of your requirements for your future mobile phone.

_____

_____

_____

_____

_____

_____

_____

_____

_____

_____

_____

_____

_____

You now have to design an A4 poster advertising your new phone using software of your choice.

Before you start, produce a couple of designs on paper. Experiment with your design before you start work on the computer. It is much easier to work with initial designs on paper.

Your poster should:

- show all the features
- be eye catching to a wide audience.

You should:

- use a background colour (this will be best if it is feint)
- be careful in your choice of colour scheme
- not use too many different font types
- use appropriate graphics
- use a border around the edges of the poster.

▶ Worksheet 3

Home entertainment anagrams

Here are some words or phrases that have been jumbled up. The words are connected with Home entertainment. Can you work out what they are? There is a clue to help you.

1 Swob err

Hint: Software you use to browse the Internet.

Answer: _____

2 Macro hot

Hint: You go into these to have conversations with others.

Answer: _____

3 Woodland

Hint: What you do to obtain files off the Internet.

Answer: _____

4 A mile

Hint: An electronic message sent between networked computers.

Answer: _____

5 Rack he

Hint: Person who gains illegal access to computer systems.

Answer: _____

6 Kilns

Hint: You take these to move between webpages and websites.

Answer: _____

7 Fir snug

Hint: Moving rapidly between webpages and websites.

Answer: _____

8 Bag weep

Hint: A page on a website.

Answer: _____

9 A tickler swooning

Hint: Facebook and MySpace are examples of this.

Answer: _____

10 Air do

Hint: Many people listen to this on the Internet whilst they are working on a computer.

Answer: _____

▶ Multiple-choice questions   pp. 16–25

1 Which of the following is a disadvantage with online betting?

A It can cause gambling addiction

B You do not have to leave the house to place a bet

C It can be done in the comfort of your own home

D You cannot get your money if you win

2 Which one of these is the input device with interactive TV?

A A remote control

B A computer keyboard

C A mouse

D A scanner

3 Which one of the following is *not* likely to be a pay-to-view service on a digital TV?

A A Premiership football match

B An important boxing match

C A very recent film

D The news

4 A digital camera is advertised as being capable of 10 megapixels.

Which one of the following statements about megapixels is incorrect?

A A megapixel is one million pixels

B A pixel is a small dot of light on the screen

C The number of megapixels will determine how clear the picture appears when displayed on the screen

D Megapixel is a unit of data storage

5 Which one of the following is an advantage of online voting?

A Not everyone has a computer connected to the Internet to vote from

B It is less effort than going out to a polling station to vote

C There are security problems with online voting

D You would have to allow some people to use paper votes

6 Interactive means which one of these?

A Conducting a two-way conversation between computer and user

B Using an input device to put data into the computer

C Using an output device to produce information

D Processing data using a computer

7 Music can be purchased and then downloaded using the Internet.

Downloaded means which one of these?

A Saving a music file

B Transferring a file from the music store to your own computer using the Internet

C Performing a virus check

D Copied illegally

8 Photographic images produced using a digital camera can be edited using which piece of software?

A Spreadsheet software

B Browser software

C Photo editing software

D Database software

9 The *main* advantage in using a digital camera compared with one with a film is which one of these?

   A You can enlarge the images
   B There is no film to develop
   C The picture quality is much higher
   D You need a scanner to input the picture

10 Software piracy involves which one of these?

   A Illegally copying computer software
   B Downloading pornography off the Internet
   C Introducing a computer virus into a computer system
   D Hacking into computer systems

ANSWERS

Questions A

▶ **TEXTBOOK PAGE 17**

1 One mark for each service to a maximum of three marks.
- Joining in with programmes by sending in comments
- See extra new stories and sports coverage
- Book cinema and holiday tickets
- Play games
- Shopping
- Placing bets
- Use email
- Place votes for programmes – there are plans to use this service for voting in parliamentary elections
- Interactive advertisements

2 (a) One mark for each component to a maximum of two marks.
- A computer/digital TV with keyboard
- Remote control
- A connection to the Internet
- Connection to digital TV service

(b) One mark for each advantage to a maximum of two marks.
- The results of elections could be obtained a lot faster
- More people would vote as they could do so without leaving their homes
- Young people would become more interested in voting if it became more high tech
- It may be cheaper, as not as many staff will be needed
- It would not be necessary to close schools in order for them to become polling stations

(c) One mark for each disadvantage to a maximum of two marks.
- Not everyone has a computer and the Internet
- Good security systems would be needed to prevent vote rigging
- It is likely to have very high initial costs

3 (a) Two marks allocated as follows:
- A conversation between the system and the person (1)
- Which allows them to make selections and pay for the bets (1)

(b) One mark for an advantage and one mark for a disadvantage.

Advantages
- You do not have to leave the house – handy for older or disabled people
- Special Internet offers – there are special offers to tempt you to gamble more
- No need to pick up your winnings – they are added to your credit or debit card
- Faster – you do not need to travel to a high street betting shop

Disadvantages
- A credit or debit card is needed – you have to create an account using a card before you are allowed to bet
- It can become addictive – for most people gambling is just a bit of fun but others can lose their family and home through excessive gambling
- People may gamble more than they would when using cash – the use of credit cards may encourage people to bet larger amounts

Questions B

▶ **TEXTBOOK PAGE 20**

1 One mark for each point to a maximum of three marks.
- One million pixels (1)
- A dot of light on the screen is a pixel (1)
- The more megapixels, the better the resolution/quality of the picture (1)

2 (a) One mark each for each distinctly different method up to a maximum of three marks.
- They can be posted onto a website or social networking site
- They can be sent by email as a file attachment
- They can be stored on CD/DVD and then given/posted
- They can be printed out
- They can be copied onto removable media

(b) One mark for each method to a maximum of two marks.
- Displayed on a computer screen
- Displayed on a mobile phone
- Printed as a hard copy using a printer
- Displayed on an electronic photo frame

3 (a) One mark for each of three reasons such as:
- No need to develop films with their high costs
- Can see the results straightaway and if the picture is not satisfactory the picture can be taken again
- You can email pictures to friends and family
- You only need to print out photographs you want, so there are no storage problems in storing lots of photographs

(b) One mark for the name or a short sentence describing each feature × 3:
- Ability to crop an image
- Ability to change the file format of an image to make it more suitable for inclusion on a website
- Ability to apply filters to an image to change the colours in the image

(c) One mark for each point to a maximum of four marks.
- A digital camera can be used to capture digital photographs (1). The images can then be inputted into the computer by attaching a cable from the camera (1) to the computer or using removable media such as magnetic media, e.g. memory cards (1)
- An ink-jet printer which has a suitable resolution that enables photographic quality printouts on paper in colour (1). Some printers can take the output from the camera in the form of memory cards or sticks and use these to input the digital images without the need for a computer (1)
- Special shiny printer paper is used with ink-jet printers to produce the best quality output of images (1)

4 (a) One mark for a description of the interface and one mark for the example × 2.
Examples of answers include:
- Steering wheel for a racing car game (1) adds to the realism making the interface between the human and computer more like the way the steering wheel is used to steer in a real racing car (1)
- Use of a joystick containing many buttons with each button controlling a certain aspect of the game. It improves the human–computer interface by making

the commands faster to issue compared to issuing commands using keys on a keyboard
(b) Two marks for a description of the nature of the problem and how it is caused.
- Playing computer games is often a sedentary activity where little physical activity takes place (1) and this can lead to obesity, which can lead to problems in later life such as stroke, heart attack (1), etc.
- Repeated use of input devices such as joysticks, a mouse (1) can lead to repetitive strain injury (RSI) which causes aching in the joints (1)
- Game players often slouch when sitting at the computer (1) and this incorrect posture when sitting can lead to back ache (1)

Questions C

▶ **TEXTBOOK PAGE 23**

1 One mark for a brief definition and one mark to a maximum of two for two things you can do using the site.
- A website where you create an online profile and add links to other profiles
- You can post personal information and inform friends what you are up to
- You can describe your interests and meet people with similar interests
- You can post photographs and videos
- You can keep in touch with friends
- You can make blog entries

2 One mark for each danger up to two marks.
- Personal information may be revealed that others can use fraudulently
- Paedophiles use these sites to look for new victims

3 One mark for each use to a maximum of two marks such as:
- You can see friends of your friends
- You can send alerts to all your friends telling them what you are up to
- You can choose your top friends
- You can meet people with interests that match your own

4 (a) One mark for each point to a maximum of two marks.
- A digital camera that is used to capture still or video images (1)
- Which can be sent to a website, saved or viewed in real time (1)
(b) One mark for each use to a maximum of two marks.
- Simple videoconferencing
- Used at tourist attractions to encourage tourists
- Used for advertising on cruise ships so you can see where they are
- Used in nurseries so parents can check up on their children whilst at work
- Used to check on the weather in different parts of the world

Questions D

▶ **TEXTBOOK PAGE 25**

1 One mark for each of two advantages such as:
- CD players are much larger and so are not as portable
- You cannot have the choice of music with a CD player as you would need to carry all the CDs
- With MP3 players you need only store the tracks you like
- It is much easier to buy tracks for an MP3 player as they can be downloaded online

2 Three tasks (one mark each) such as:
- Send and receive text messages
- Take digital photographs
- Take short video clips
- Surf the Internet
- Watch live TV
- Send and receive email
- Download and listen to music
- Download and play games
- Send picture messages
- Play videos
- GPS (use your mobile phone as a satellite navigation system)

3 (a) One mark to a maximum of four for points similar to the following:
- By using the Internet music files can be used off websites if copyright permissions allow
- The development of removable storage media has meant that music files are easily transferred between devices
- Compression techniques mean music files can be reduced in size, which means that more of them can be stored in the same place
- Compression of files means that they are uploaded or downloaded using the Internet in a short period of time
(b) One mark for an ethical issue and one mark for a legal issue.
- Ethical – people loading digital music on many different devices that are used simultaneously against the licence agreement
- Legal – file sharing sites encouraging users to share their music files with each other rather than buying

Test yourself

▶ **TEXTBOOK PAGE 26**

A interactive
B Pay-to-view
C vote
D digital
E photo editing
F gaming
G input / webcam
H download / MP3
I Social

Examination style questions

▶ **TEXTBOOK PAGE 27**

1 One mark for a danger such as:
- Paedophiles may use webcams to view their victims (1)
- Webcam sites may promote terrorism, violence, etc. (1)
- Some webcam sites contain pornography (1)

2 One mark for each point to a maximum of five marks.
- If a picture is taken and is no good it can be deleted and taken again (1)
- Large numbers of pictures can be stored on a small memory card (1)
- It encourages people to experiment with new effects (1)
- Photographs can be edited using photo editing software (1)
- Photographs can be taken using mobile phones (1)
- Photographs can be sent from one phone to another (1)
- Photographs can be attached to an email to a friend or a group of friends (1)
- It is very easy to copy digital images onto portable storage devices (1)

- Photographs can be published on websites where they can be copied by friends (1)
- Photographs can be put onto social networking sites (1)

3 One mark each for two examples such as:

Some recent films (1)

Premiership matches or boxing matches (1)

Popular old films (1)

4 (a) One mark for each point to a maximum of two marks.
- An image sensor picks up the light from the image (1)
- The image sensor is made up of a silicon chip consisting of millions of photosensitive diodes (1)
- Each diode is capable of capturing a pixel of light in the photograph to be (1)
- The pixels form the whole picture (1)
- The whole map of the pixels is converted to a binary code (1) and this is compressed before storing (1)

(b) One mark for one point such as:
- Reduces the file size so more can be stored on the memory card (1)
- It enables them to be sent over a phone service or the Internet in less time (1)

(c) One mark for one medium such as:
- Memory card (1)
- Memory stick (1)
- Picture card (1)
- Flash memory (1)
- Pen drive (1)

(d) One mark for one output device such as:
- A computer screen
- A printer (ink-jet printers are the best types for printing photographs)
- A TV (some TVs have memory card readers)
- The screen of a mobile phone
- A digital photo frame

5 (a) One mark each for three descriptions that clearly outline the impact. One mark for the clarity of expression. Example answers for this include:
- Online games – enables children to learn about the world around them and teaches them to follow instructions
- Use of the Internet for homework – teaches children valuable information searching skills that will be useful in later life and at work
- Using instant messaging and emails – teaches children to form friendships with others their own age and teaches them valuable communication skills and encourages them to write

(b) One mark for each problem and one mark for the example × 2.
- Health problems such as RSI, back ache and eye strain through constant use of computer equipment. Parents need to encourage children to use good practice when working with computers such as sitting up straight, not using laptops when laying on the floor, etc.
- Problems with children accessing chat rooms without their parents' knowledge and arranging to meet others who may do them harm. Parents should not let young children use the Internet without parental supervision

6 Three marks for three advantages and three marks for three disadvantages such as:

Advantages
- Communication any place any time
- People can be contacted when on the move
- Enables people to make plans or change plans at the last minute

- Can be used for surfing the Internet when not near a computer

Disadvantages
- Employees who have been supplied with mobile phones from their company may feel they are never away from work
- Others may be disturbed by the ringing of mobiles on public transport or in restaurants
- People may feel their privacy is eroded by mobile phone companies keeping information about their phone conversations

---

Worksheet 1: The Internet: What do these terms mean?

▶ **TEACHER'S RESOURCE GUIDE TOPIC 2 PAGE 13**

Term	Meaning
Browser	Software used to search for information using the Internet.
Chat room	A virtual meeting place where you can have online conversations with other people.
Cookie	A small program that monitors your searching activity.
Download	Obtaining a file off the Internet and saving it on your own computer.
Email	A electronic message sent over a network which is usually the Internet.
FAQ	Frequently Ask Questions: A list of the questions the people who use a website most often ask along with the answers.
Hacker	A person who gains illegal access to a computer system.
HTML	A list of instructions on how to display the content of a webpage.
ISP	Internet service provider. The people who provide you with your Internet connection.
Link	A way of moving from one place to another on the Internet.
Modem	A device used to send and receive signals over the Internet.
Surfing	Moving around different webpages and websites using the links on the Internet.
User-ID	A name given to you or that you give yourself so that you are recognized by the system.
Webpage	A document/page that has been uploaded to enable it to be accessed by anyone using the Internet.

Worksheet 3: Home entertainment anagrams

▶ **TEACHER'S RESOURCE GUIDE TOPIC 2 PAGE 15**

1 Browser
2 Chat room
3 Download
4 Email
5 Hacker
6 Links
7 Surfing
8 Webpage
9 Social networking
10 Radio

Multiple-choice questions

▶ **TEACHER'S RESOURCE GUIDE TOPIC 2 PAGE 16**

1A, 2A, 3D, 4D, 5B, 6A, 7B, 8C, 9B, 10A

▶ Worksheet pp. 32–35

Home and personal communication systems anagrams

Here are some words or phrases that have been jumbled up. The words are connected with Home and personal communication systems. Can you work out what they are? There is a clue to help you.

1 Swirl see   *Hint: Without wires.*

Answer: _____

2 Little sea   *Hint: In orbit.*

Answer: _____

3 Stop hot   *Hint: A place where you can get wireless Internet.*

Answer: _____

4 Barb add on   *Hint: Fast Internet connection.*

Answer: _____

5 Hotel bout   *Hint: Way of connecting devices.*

Answer: _____

6 Chirp gala   *Hint: Type of information system.*

Answer: _____

7 Retire slow sure   *Hint: A device used to allow wireless access to the Internet.*

Answer: _____

8 Woodland   *Hint: Way of getting music off the Internet.*

Answer: _____

9 Brewery slide soak   *Hint: A keyboard without wires.*

Answer: _____

10 Screen mean   *Hint: Your Internet name.*

Answer: _____

▶ Activity 1

p. 32

Wireless Internet

Many people who use the Internet do not want to be restricted by cables. They want to be able to access the Internet wirelessly wherever they are.

Imagine that you are employed in a job where you have a very busy schedule and have to do a lot of travelling.

For this activity you have to produce an advert that advertises a phone or notebook computer that can be used for Internet access. The emphasis in your advert must be on those features that will make the device as portable as possible and give very fast access to the Internet.

Make sure that your advert targets the busy person who is always on the move.
You are free to choose whatever software you think would be best for this task.

▶ **Activity 2** pp. 34–35

Researching geographical information systems

For this activity you have to do some research on geographical information systems.

You need to find out and write a short case study on two applications of geographical information systems.

▶ Multiple-choice questions

1 **The main advantage in using broadband, compared to using a modem, is which of the following?**

A It is cheaper to buy
B It allows faster transfer of data
C You can use email
D You can download files

2 **To watch video over the Internet you need which of the following types of connection?**

A Bandlength
B Bandwidth
C Modem
D Broadband

3 **Bluetooth is which of the following?**

A A way of devices communicating with each other
B An infected tooth
C An Internet service provider
D A device that allows several computers to access the Internet at the same time

4 **Which one of the following statements about Bluetooth is incorrect?**

A It uses radio signals
B It can only be used over short distances
C It can communicate directly with satellites
D It can be used for wireless control of devices

5 **Bluetooth is said to have a low bandwidth.**

Which one of the following best describes what the consequence of this is?

A Data is not sent as quickly
B It is easy to set up
C You do not need wires to make a connection
D Data is sent very quickly

6 **Which one of the following tasks can only properly be done using broadband?**

A Sending an email
B Connecting to the Internet
C Downloading a file
D Watching an online video

7 **A region where the Internet can be accessed wirelessly is called which of these?**

A An Internet café
B A hotspot
C A blog spot
D A hop spot

8 **Which one of the following best describes the term broadband?**

A A dialup Internet connection
B A slow connection to the Internet
C A fast connection to the Internet
D The software you use to search the Internet

9 **Satellite communication is used for which of the following?**

A For short distance communication
B To enable long distance communication across continents
C To connect Bluetooth devices
D To connect a computer using dialup

10 **GIS stands for which one of these?**

A Graphic information system
B Geographical information system
C Graphic interface system
D Graphic input system

ANSWERS

Questions A

▶ **TEXTBOOK PAGE 33**

1 One mark each for the answers:
   - Dialup
   - Broadband
2 One mark for each advantage to a maximum of two marks.
   - No wires to sink/conceal
   - Can work anywhere in the office or even outside close to the office
   - Easier to keep the offices clean
   - Fewer trailing wires to trip over
3 One mark for
   They may be worried that hackers may gain access to the network
4 One mark for each of two tasks such as:
   - Download files at high speed
   - Watch online video
   - Use web cameras
   - Listen to online radio
   - Watch TV programmes
   - Surf the Internet very quickly

Questions B

▶ **TEXTBOOK PAGE 35**

1 (a) One mark for each name in a suitable pair of devices such as:
   - Keyboard and computer
   - Mouse and computer
   - Mobile phone and computer
   - Camera and computer
   - Computer and printer
   - Etc.
   (b) One mark for an advantage such as:
   - No direct connection is needed so it is easier
   - No need to hunt for a cable to make the connection
   (c) One mark for a disadvantage such as:
   - Bluetooth only has a short range, which limits its use
   - There is a danger of hackers accessing the system
2 One mark for the use and one mark for further description of the use × 2.
   - Satellite navigation systems (1) allow you to find tourist destinations when on holiday (1)
   - Google Earth (1) – you can view the area surrounding a hotel you are thinking of booking abroad (1)
3 One mark for each disadvantage to a maximum of two marks.
   - They sometimes get confused and give the wrong directions
   - They can send you on inappropriate routes
   - Drivers sometimes enter details when they are driving which is dangerous

Test yourself

▶ **TEXTBOOK PAGE 36**

A Satellites
B wireless
C Modems
D Dialup

E Cable
F router
G Bluetooth
H GIS
I synchronize

Examination style questions

▶ **TEXTBOOK PAGE 36**

1 (a) Two marks allocated as follows:
   A huge group of networks (1) linked together (1)
   (b) One mark each to a maximum of two marks.
   - A dialup modem
   - A network card
   - A cable/wire
   - A wireless router
   - A broadband connection (accept cable modem)
   (c) One mark for the definition and one mark each for two advantages.
   - High speed access to the Internet via cable or wireless (1)
   - Offers high speed download and upload of data (1)
   - Can browse websites at high speed (1)
   - Can watch real-time video (1)
   - Can listen to radio programmes as you work (1)
2 (a) One mark for each point to a maximum of two marks such as:
   - Several people may be using a single connection to the Internet, so the speed is shared between them
   - There may be a lot of users online at the same time, which slows the whole system down
   - There may be a virus which is slowing your system down
   - You may have lots of different applications open at the same time
   (b) One mark for the name and one mark for further description or an example × 2.
   - Download files at high speed (1) – you can download music or films using your Internet connection (1)
   - Watch online video (1) – for example, watching i-Player or YouTube would be impossible without broadband (1)
   - Use web cameras (1) – can chat to people and see them at the same time (1)
   - Listen to online radio (1) – you can listen real time or to programmes you missed when they were broadcast (1)
   - Watch TV programmes (1) – can use the BBC i-Player (1)
   - Surf the Internet very quickly (1) – dialup takes ages just to get a connection (1)
3 Two marks for an answer similar to the following:
   - Broadband is a lot faster so webpages on the Internet will not take long to load (1)
   - With broadband you do not have to wait for the system to make a connection (1)
4 One mark for each of two applications.
   - To allow hardware (e.g., mouse, keyboard, etc.) to communicate wirelessly with the computer
   - For printing a page using a computer that is not connected via a wire to a printer
   - To allow a hands-free headset to be used with a mobile phone when driving a car

Worksheet: Home and personal communication systems anagrams

▶ **TEACHER'S RESOURCE GUIDE TOPIC 3 PAGE 22**

1 Wireless
2 Satellite
3 Hotspot
4 Broadband
5 Bluetooth
6 Graphical
7 Wireless router
8 Download
9 Wireless keyboard
10 Screen name

Multiple-choice questions

▶ **TEACHER'S RESOURCE GUIDE TOPIC 3 PAGE 25**

1B, 2D, 3A, 4C, 5A, 6D, 7B, 8C, 9B, 10B

▶ Worksheet

Home business anagrams

Here are some words or phrases that have been jumbled up. The words are connected with Home business. Can you work out what they are? There is a clue to help you.

1 Inert ten   *Hint: The largest network of networks in the world.*

Answer: _____

2 Edit tiny   *Hint: People can steal this if you are not careful when making online purchases.*

Answer: _____

3 Tin up   *Hint: The data being put into the computer.*

Answer: _____

4 Saws drops   *Hint: Used to ensure that a person is who they say they are when using the Internet.*

Answer: _____

5 Fair eviction   *Hint: Visually checking that the details you have input into the computer are correct.*

Answer: _____

6 Cry den pet   *Hint: Card details are _____ before being transferred over the Internet.*

Answer: _____

7 Direct   *Hint: Many adults have one of these cards.*

Answer: _____

8 Chaser   *Hint: A quick way to find goods on an online site.*

Answer: _____

9 Task be   *Hint: You can put your online shopping in one.*

Answer: _____

10 Sic um   *Hint: One of the most frequently downloaded products.*

Answer: _____

▶ Activity

Investigating online shopping sites

Many people now shop online.

For this activity you are required to browse the following sites, some of which you may already be familiar with.

Here are the sites you need to look at:

http://www.amazon.co.uk/

http://www.asos.com/

http://www.tesco.com/

Produce a list of the things you like about these online sites and also a list of the things you do not like about them.

Please note that you are comparing the sites and how easy they are to use and not the range of products they are selling.

▶ Multiple-choice questions pp. 40–44

1 Online shopping using the Internet is often called which of these?

A E-commerce
B Bluetooth
C Email
D Wi-fi

2 Which of the following is *not* an advantage of online shopping?

A The goods are usually cheaper
B Some traditional shops may have to close
C Orders can be placed at any time of the day
D There is a much bigger choice of products

3 When creating a user account a password is created and this is typed in twice.

Which one of the following is the main reason for this?

A To verify the password by checking that the user has not made any errors in typing a password
B To ensure that only numbers are entered
C To validate that the person trying to gain access is who they say they are
D To waste time

4 Booking flights online is usually cheaper than booking over the phone. Part of the reason for this is which one of these?

A Phone calls are expensive
B The customer inputs their own data, so fewer staff are needed
C The plane does not need to carry as much fuel as the tickets are lighter
D The tickets are paid for using a credit or debit card

5 Online stores have a checkout. Which one of the following statements about checkout is incorrect?

A Checkout is where a customer pays for their goods
B Checkout involves the customer entering payment details
C Checkout involves the customer giving their name and address details
D Checkout is where the goods are put into the basket

6 Which one of the following is *not* a method of searching for a holiday online?

A Using a menu
B Browsing
C Clicking on links
D Asking for assistance in the travel agent's office

▶ Multiple-choice questions
(continued)

7 **Which one of the following is a feature of an online booking site and *not* a paper-based brochure?**

A Virtual tours of the hotel and surroundings

B Tables of prices at different times of the year

C Photographs of the hotel

D A list of the hotel facilities

8 **Which one is *not* an advantage to a holiday company of online booking?**

A Fewer staff needed

B Can locate premises anywhere

C The equipment needed is expensive

D Can operate 24 hours per day everyday

9 **Which one of the following is *not* an advantage in using an online site to book a holiday?**

A It is possible to book 24/7

B It is quicker to find alternatives if the holiday you wanted is fully booked

C It is easier to shop around

D You have to be careful to enter the correct dates

10 **Which one of the following is an advantage of a bookstore selling its books online?**

A Customers may be put off entering their debit/credit card details

B The customer gets the book delivered to their home

C There are fewer overheads in trading online

D You do not have the problem of people browsing but not buying

ANSWERS

Questions A

▶ **TEXTBOOK PAGE 42**

1 (a) One method for one mark such as:
- Credit card
- Debit card
- PayPal

(b) One mark for each point to a maximum of two marks.
- They are worried about identity theft (1)
- They are worried that their card details could be used fraudulently (1)

(c) One mark for each point to a maximum of two marks.
- Credit/debit card details are encrypted (1)
- Which means they are put into a secret code (1)
- Which prevents others understanding them (1)

2 (a) One mark for each correct answer (7 marks in total).

Task	Facility needed
To allow lots of items to be selected for purchase	Shopping basket
To allow customers to enter their payment details safely	Encryption
To allow customers to browse the e-commerce site at high speed	Broadband
To allow the details of customers and their orders to be kept by the e-commerce site	Online database
To allow customers to view all the items for sale	Website
To allow customers to access other websites that may be of interest	Links
To communicate with customers about problems with their order	Email

(b) (i) One mark for a description similar to:
- File is transferred from the store website to the shopper's computer via the Internet
- The distribution costs are much lower

(ii) One mark for answers similar to the following:
- No packing and postage needed

(iii) One mark for answers similar to the following:
- They get their goods almost instantly
- Downloads are cheaper because there are no CDs to produce

3 (a) One mark each for two advantages such as:
- The goods are usually cheaper
- It is much easier to shop around
- You can use comparison sites to get the best price
- You can see what others say about the service offered by the online store
- The goods are delivered straight to your door
- You can buy goods from anywhere in the world
- You do not waste time looking for goods that might be out of stock

(b) One mark each for two disadvantages such as:
- If you want the goods urgently you may still have to wait for delivery
- It is sometimes necessary to see and touch what you are buying
- It is hassle sending goods back
- Sometime the customer service is not as good as a traditional store

- There are fake stores where you pay for goods that never arrive
- People may be worried about using their credit/debit card details to pay for goods owing to identity theft

(c) (i) One mark each for two suitable stores such as:
- Supermarkets
- Clothes stores
- Bookshops
- CD/DVD stores

(ii) One mark each for two similar to
- High street bookshops
- High street record stores
- Corner shops
- High street travel agents

4 One mark for each detailed point (not just a name) to a maximum of six.
- Goods or services are usually cheaper on the Internet. Organizations find it cheaper to use the Internet, as they do not need as many staff, they do not need expensive premises and some of these savings can be passed to the customer.
- Online catalogues can be viewed. Products can be searched for by a large number of criteria.
- There is much bigger choice of products. Internet bookshops have huge stocks of books compared to a local bookshop.
- Product reviews can be obtained before you buy. For example, you can see what other people, who have bought a book, say about it before you buy.
- Orders can be placed on the Internet 24 hours a day, 7 days a week, 52 weeks per year.
- You can buy software/music over the Internet and receive it by downloading it. This can be less effort than having to order it by mail order or by travelling to a shop to buy it.
- You can use price comparison sites to ensure that the goods are bought for the best price.
- Once the customer has made an initial order, the customer details such as name, address, credit card details are stored and therefore do not need to be entered. This makes shopping online very fast. Supermarkets who deliver to the home also keep a shopping list of items that you order regularly so you just need to make changes in this list.
- You can buy goods anywhere in the world.

Questions B

▶ **TEXTBOOK PAGE 44**

1 (a) One mark for each point similar to the following up to six marks:
- The customer enters the URL/website address of the site into the browser
- The customer searches for the site using a search engine and then follows the link
- The customer enters the details of departure and arrival airports
- They enter the date they want to go
- They enter the number of nights
- The customer browses all the holidays shown
- The customer can look at virtual tours of the hotel and surroundings
- The customer can view reviews
- The customer selects the holiday

- They enter their details such as number of passengers, names and addresses
- They enter options for flights and hotel (e.g., in-flight meals, seats with extra legroom, etc.)
- They enter the payment details such as credit/debit card numbers
- They verify any information they enter visually by comparing with the actual documents (e.g., credit card, etc.)
- They receive a confirmation email
- They print out the email which may act as tickets

(b) One mark each for two points such as:
- You have to enter credit/debit card details and these may not be kept safe
- People could hack into the site and know you were away and burgle your house
- There is no personal service like at a high street travel agent
- You could easily enter the wrong information and book the wrong flights

2 (a) One mark for each point to a maximum of two marks.
- They are less likely to make a mistake when inputting their own details
- They are responsible if a mistake has been made
- They are more likely to spot a mistake about themselves
- You do not have to pay people to input the details so it is cheaper

(b) One mark for each point to a maximum of two marks.
- They would perform a visual check/proof read
- By comparing what they have typed in with documents (e.g., date could be checked with a calendar, credit card details checked against the actual card, etc.)
- Check for spelling mistakes in names, etc.

Test yourself

▶ **TEXTBOOK PAGE 45**

A Online
B debit
C identity
D music, downloaded
E Internet
F input
G verify, visual
H Passwords

Examination style questions

▶ **TEXTBOOK PAGE 46**

1 (a) One mark for each correct item of data to a maximum of three marks.
- Departure and arrival airport
- Date of departure and date of arrival
- Number of travellers
- Name of resort
- Name of accommodation
- Payment details/credit/debit card details

(b) One mark each for two answers similar to the following:
- You are not as hurried/pressured as when you are booking through a high street travel agent
- You can get a cheaper deal, as the costs for the online business are lower
- You do not have to waste time travelling to a travel agent

- Others in different part of the country can see the information if you are going to be booking together

(c) One mark each for two answers similar to the following:
- You have to enter payment details, which could be used fraudulently
- You could easily make mistakes and lose your holiday
- Others could find out when you are away and your house could be burgled
- Not everyone has a computer and access to the Internet
- Some people would prefer the personal service of a travel agent

2 (a) One mark for an answer similar to:
File is transferred from the store website to the shopper's computer via the Internet

(b) One mark for each product to a maximum of two marks.
- Music
- Films/video
- Software
- Photographs (from an image library)

(c) One mark for each point to a maximum of four marks. Note that this is a discuss question so should be answered in sentences.
- You can get the goods instantly
- They are in a form you can use instantly/you do not have to convert music on CD to MP3 format to use with your portable music player
- They are cheaper
- You only have to pay for certain tracks
- If you get fed up with a CD you can sell it but with downloads you cannot do this
- You do not have the information on the sleeve like you do with a CD
- There is always a danger in introducing viruses when downloading files

3 One mark for each correct answer (7 marks in total)

Task	Facility needed
Go straight to a product if you know a description	Search
A place to put items you want to buy	Shopping cart
A fast Internet connection that allows you to browse quickly	Broadband
The system to ensure the security of credit/debit card details	Encryption
You can see what others say before you buy	Customer reviews
The place where you pay for goods	Checkout
The basis of the online catalogue of goods for sale	Database

4 (a) One advantage for one mark such as:
- Can shop interactively without the need for a computer
- Whole family can see clearly the goods on offer before buying
- Can shop direct from living room without the need for a laptop

(b) One disadvantage for one mark such as:
- You could be persuaded by programmes to buy things you do not really need

- It is too easy to make quick decisions about purchases you may regret later
- Some people run up large credit card amounts which they cannot pay off

5 One mark for each point to a maximum of five marks. This is a discuss question so the answer needs to be written in complete sentences like the one shown here. The marks allocated are shown in brackets.

More and more people are able to access the Internet via their computers, interactive digital TV, mobile phones, etc. (1). All these users will now be able to take advantage of online sites and be able to buy their goods and services cheaper (1) and more efficiently than before (1). As well as needing the hardware and software to access the Internet, the user will also need a credit card to pay for their purchases (1). One problem is that the well off people will be able to take advantage of the savings whereas the less well off (who will not be able to afford to have access to the Internet or will not be able to get a credit card) will lose out (1).

Worksheet: Home business anagrams

▶ **TEACHER'S RESOURCE GUIDE TOPIC 4 PAGE 28**

 1 Internet
 2 Identity
 3 Input
 4 Password
 5 Verification
 6 Encrypted
 7 Credit
 8 Search
 9 Basket
10 Music

Multiple-choice questions

▶ **TEACHER'S RESOURCE GUIDE TOPIC 4 PAGE 30**

1A, 2B, 3A, 4B, 5D, 6D, 7A, 8C, 9D, 10C

▶ Worksheet 1 | pp. 52–61

Organizations: school, home and environment anagrams

Here are some words or phrases that have been jumbled up. The words are connected with Organizations: school, home and environment. Can you work out what they are? There is a clue to help you.

1 Competition coral ark gin *Hint: Data input method.*

Answer: _____

2 Scram dart *Hint: Card containing a chip.*

Answer: _____

3 Cider wasp *Hint: Card with a stripe on it.*

Answer: _____

4 Orbit mice *Hint: Such as fingerprinting or retinal scanning.*

Answer: _____

5 Long gig *Hint: Taking readings automatically.*

Answer: _____

6 Fret grin gin pin *Hint: Biometric method.*

Answer: _____

7 Rail ten *Hint: Scanning of the eye.*

Answer: _____

8 Magic net *Hint: Type of strip on a swipe card.*

Answer: _____

9 Magnet name *Hint: Type of information system used in a business.*

Answer: _____

10 Goal grin get *Hint: The frequency of taking readings in a data logging experiment.*

Answer: _____

▶ Worksheet 2 | pp. 57–59

Computers in control?

There are many places where you can find computers in control. Computers can switch things on and off automatically. They can work through a process without the need for a human to be present.

Name three examples under each category. Write your answers directly onto the worksheet. Example 1 has been completed for you.

Place where you might find computers in control	Example 1	Example 2	Example 3
In your school	Central heating system		
In your home	Washing machine		
At a fairground/theme park	To count people passing through the turnstiles		
Along a road	Fog warning system		
In a shopping centre	Controlling the barrier in the car park		

Describing how control is used

There are many places where control is used. For this worksheet you have to explain how control is used for each of the examples described.
To make it clear what you have to do, the first example has been done for you.

Place where you might find computers in control	Example	How control is used
In your school	Central heating system	*To turn the heating on when the temperature, as measured by a sensor, falls below a set value. If the temperature rises above a different set value, and the heating is on, then it will be turned off. This way the temperature remains fairly constant.*
In your home	Washing machine	
At a fairground/ theme park	To count people passing through the turnstiles	
Along a road	Fog warning system	
In a shopping centre	Controlling the barrier in the car park	

⏵ **Extension activity** | p. 54

School management information systems

There are many companies that supply school management information systems.

Your task is to find out a little more about the tasks that they can perform. Here are a couple of their websites:

http://www.capitaes.co.uk/sims/
http://www.bromcom.com/

Write a list of things that these management information systems do to make the running of a school easier.

⏵ **Extension activity** | p. 54

▶ Activity

p. 54

Planning a student record

You have to think about the information a school needs to hold about you.

Work in small groups to produce a student record input screen that the school staff can use to input student details. Make sure that the important information is at the top of the screen as this is needed the most often.

Produce a final 'group' input screen design and hand it in to your teacher.

▶ Multiple-choice questions | pp. 52–61

1 **Instead of entering the student number 009089, the user mistypes in the incorrect number 009098. This is an example of which kind of error?**

A A parity error
B A transposition error
C A transcription error
D A range error

2 **Collecting data at regular intervals over a set period of time is called which of these?**

A Data logging
B Data processing
C Data communications
D Data validation

3 **The main advantage of data logging is which of these?**

A Readings can be taken automatically
B The readings are more accurate
C Computing equipment is needed
D No expensive equipment is needed

4 **An experiment is conducted to see which cup holds heat the best. Coffee at the same temperature is poured into the two cups made of different thickness of polystyrene. A temperature sensor is inserted in each cup and the data is logged over a period.**

What would be the most suitable logging interval for the temperature measurements (i.e., the time between measurements)?

A 1 minute
B 1 hour
C 1 day
D 1 week

5 **An experiment is conducted to see which cup holds heat the best. Coffee at the same temperature is poured into the two cups made of different thickness of polystyrene. A temperature sensor is inserted in each cup and the data is logged over a period.**

What would be the most suitable logging period (i.e., the total time for all the measurements)?

A 1 minute
B 5 minutes
C 30 minutes
D 5 hours

6 **The logging period is which of these?**

A The time the computer is switched on for
B The time over which the measurements are made
C How often the individual readings are taken
D A record that the operating system keeps

7 The logging interval is which of these?

A The time between the readings
B The time the computer is switched on for
C The time a program takes to load
D The wait to log onto the Internet

8 Here is a short program written in the programming language LOGO.

FORWARD 10
RIGHT 90
FORWARD 10
RIGHT 90
FORWARD 10
RIGHT 90
FORWARD 10

The shape drawn by this program is which of these?

A A rectangle
B A triangle
C A cube
D A square

9 The system of registration that involves the teacher marking students' attendance by shading in boxes using a pencil is called which one of these?

A Optical character recognition
B Bar coding
C Optical mark recognition
D Fingerprinting

10 Some school attendance systems give each student a smart card. A smart card always contains which one of these?

A A bar code
B A chip
C A magnetic strip
D A fingerprint scanner

ANSWERS

Questions A

▶ **TEXTBOOK PAGE 53**

1 (a) One mark each for three advantages such as:
- The details are recorded instantly – teachers and admin staff can chase up non-attendees
- Teachers have the admin burden removed – they can concentrate on teaching
- Harder for students to abuse the system
- Promotes health and safety – need to know who is in the school in case of an emergency
- Can check attendance at each lesson
- No need to physically move the registers
- Takes up less space than paper-based registers
- Attendance records can be accessed from any computer connected to the school network

(b) One mark for each of three disadvantages such as:
- The cost – biometric methods are quite expensive
- Dependence on equipment that can sometimes fail
- Privacy issues if fingerprinting is used

2 (a) One mark for one of the following:
- Retinal scanning/retina pattern/eye pattern, etc.
- Fingerprinting

(b) One mark for the name/brief description and one mark for detail of the advantage.
- Quicker – teachers no longer have to register them
- Cannot abuse the system – students cannot mark in for someone else
- Gives the exact time – can tell exactly how late each student is
- Operates in real time – system immediately records student attending

Questions B

▶ **TEXTBOOK PAGE 54**

1 (a) One mark for management information system.
(b) One mark for a suitable advantage such as:
- They reduce the workload for teachers in the classroom and in the school office
- They can provide up-to-date information for parents
- They can support decision making for school managers
- They can tackle truancy effectively
- They can be used to plan timetables
- They can be used to help make budgeting decisions

(c) One mark for a suitable disadvantage such as:
- The software is expensive to buy
- Student data is personal, so there must be no unauthorized access
- Software is complex, so all staff need training

2 (a) Two marks allocated as follows:
An ICT system that supplies managers and other staff (1) with the information they need in order to make decisions (1)

(b) Two marks allocated in a similar way to the following example:
A head teacher using information from feeder primary schools and other data (1) to work out how many students there are likely to be in the new intake of Year 7 (1) to decide if they have enough staff and resources (1)

Activity: Which sensor?

▶ **TEXTBOOK PAGE 56**

1 One mark for temperature/heat sensor
2 One mark for explanation and one mark for further amplification or an example.
The frequency with which the temperature readings are taken (1), for example every 30 seconds, every minute, etc. (1)
3 One mark for 'per minute'.
4 One mark for explanation and one mark for further amplification or an example.
The time over which the entire experiment is conducted/ the total time for which all the readings are taken (1). For example, one hour, one day, one week, etc. (1)
5 One mark for 1 hour
6 One mark for an answer similar to:
This will be near to the time taken for the temperature of the hot drink to cool to near room temperature.

Questions C

▶ **TEXTBOOK PAGE 56**

1 (a) One mark for temperature/heat sensor
(b) One mark for an answer similar to:
The sensors take each measurement and send it to the data logger
(c) One mark for 24 hours
(d) One mark for a correct definition and sensible logging interval.
Example answer:
It is the frequency with which the temperature readings are taken (1)
The temperature could be taken every hour (1)

2 (a) One mark for the name and one mark for a description of what it does × 2.
- Moisture (1) – so that the amount of water in the soil can be determined in case it is too dry (1)
- Humidity (1) – the moisture in the air can be measured so that a fine mist can be turned on or off
- Light (1) – the light is measured and controls the blinds (1)
- pH (1) – to control the acidity/alkalinity of the soil (1)

(b) One mark for each advantage to a maximum of two marks.
- The system is completely automatic (1)
- No wage costs for people to water plants (1)

(c) One mark for one disadvantage such as:
- High initial cost of buying the equipment
- Equipment needs to be maintained
- Equipment can malfunction which can cause plant loss
- Causes unemployment among staff who used to look after plants manually

Questions D

▶ **TEXTBOOK PAGE 59**

1 Marks according to the following.
No mistakes in instructions = 4 marks
1 mistake = 3 marks

2–3 mistakes = 2 marks
4–5 mistakes = 1 mark
>5 mistakes = 0 marks
FORWARD 50
RIGHT 90
FORWARD 25
PENUP
FORWARD 50
PENDOWN
FORWARD 25
RIGHT 90
FORWARD 50
RIGHT 90
FORWARD 100

2 (a) One mark for 'all the conditions are ideal'
   (b) One mark for 'the temperature and light are too high'
   (c) One mark for 'the humidity and the moisture are too high'
   (d) One mark for 'the temperature and humidity are too high'

3 One mark for each point made in the explanation up to a maximum of two marks.
   • Pressure pad on the floor (1) so that when someone stands on it the automatic door opens (1)
   • Pads on the floor around the school (1) so that when an intruder steps on them the burglar alarm is sounded (1)
   • Pads on the floor near the reception area (1) so that the staff can be alerted by a bell that there is someone waiting (1)

Questions E

▶ TEXTBOOK PAGE 61

1 (a) Two marks for two points such as:
   • Readings are taken regularly (1)
   • Readings are taken automatically (1)
   • Using sensors (1)
   • Data is stored/communicated to a computer where it is processed (1)
   (b) One mark each for three weather quantities such as:
   • Pressure
   • Humidity
   • Rainfall/precipitation/snow
   • Wind speed
   • Wind direction
   • Sunshine

2 (a) One mark for each advantage to a maximum of three marks.
   • Data can be collected automatically – no human needed so cheaper
   • Data is collected at exactly the correct time
   • Mistakes are not made when taking readings – no human error
   • Weather data can be collected from remote and inhospitable locations
   • Data can be transmitted using radio/satellite communication
   (b) One mark for one disadvantage such as:
   • Equipment is expensive
   • Malfunction of equipment may lead to incorrect forecasts
   (c) One mark each for logging period and logging rate.
   • Logging period is the time over which all the readings are taken
   • Logging rate is how frequently each reading is taken (e.g., every minute, every hour, etc.)

3 (a) One mark for a situation such as:
   • Recording temperature to find out about global warming (1)
   • Working out the average monthly temperature at a holiday resort (1)
   (b) One mark for a reason such as:
   • A lot less expensive than having a human present to take reading
   • Readings are taken at exactly the correct time
   • Accurate readings are always taken/no human error

Case study

▶ TEXTBOOK PAGE 62

1 (a) One mark for each point to a maximum of two marks.
   • Uses a unique property of the human body (1)
   • Scans fingerprints and matches the pattern to one stored (1)
   • Used to identify a particular person (1)
   (b) One mark for an answer such as:
   • You do not need to remember a card
   • You do not need to spend time finding a card in your bag
   • It is much faster than other methods
   • It is less open to abuse because you have to be present yourself
   (c) One mark for each point similar to the following:
   • No full fingerprints are stored (1)
   • Fingerprints are stored as a code (1)
   • You cannot recreate the fingerprints from this code (1)

2 One mark each for two answers such as:
   • Fingerprint data is personal data and should have appropriate security measures that schools may not be able to provide
   • Fingerprint data could be passed to outside organizations such as the police

Test yourself

▶ TEXTBOOK PAGE 63

A optical mark reading
B swipe
C biometric
D retinal
E management information system
F sensors
G period
H data logging

Examination style questions

▶ TEXTBOOK PAGE 63

1 (a) Two sensors (one mark each) such as:
   • Pressure
   • Temperature
   • Humidity
   • Rainfall
   • Light/Sun – to record hours of sunlight
   (b) One mark for a method and one mark for further amplification.
   • The data is sent wirelessly (1) through the air and it is picked up by a receiver inside or attached to the computer (1)
   (c) One mark for a method and an extra mark for further detail.

- It is displayed on a small LCD screen (1) in the form of icons (such as sun/rain, etc.) (1)
- It is displayed graphically (1)
- Graphs are drawn to show the way the quantity measured has changed (1)

2 (a) One mark for the name of a suitable device such as:
- Washing machine
- Dishwasher
- Iron
- Toaster
- Alarm

(b) One mark for each point to a maximum of three marks. Example answer for a washing machine control system might be:
- Controls the flow of water into the machine
- Heats the water up to the correct temperature
- Uses the program to obey the set of instructions for a particular wash
- Controls the pumps that pump the dirty water out of the machine
- Controls when the detergent is added
- Controls the spin speed
- Controls how long the drier cycle is on for
- Releases the door hatch when it is safe to do so

3 (a) One mark for each of two points similar to the following:
- Pattern of blood vessels at the back of the eye/on the retina is unique (1)
- The retina is scanned and the pattern is used to match with pre-stored patterns (1) in a database with other details (1) and this is passed to the attendance system which marks the student in (1)

(b) One mark for each of two points:
- They can get a list of students who have not attended after every registration (1)
- They can ring up/text/email parents to find the reason why they are not there (1)
- This discourages students from not attending because they will know that they will be caught (1)
- Students who arrive late can be identified for further investigation (1)

(c) One mark for each point to a maximum of two marks.
- The system is expensive to buy (1)
- The equipment is sophisticated and can break down (1)
- Staff and students will need to be trained on how to use the new system (1)
- Students could vandalize the reader (1)

4 (a) One mark for each point to a maximum of two marks.
- ICT system that makes use of a unique property of the human body (1)
- Such as fingerprints or the pattern on the retina (1)
- That can be used to match against previously stored information so that the person can be identified (1)

(b) One mark for each point to a maximum of two marks:
- Paper-based registers (1) where marks are made on paper and these are processed manually (1)
- Teachers have to add up totals (1)
- Registers are returned at the end of each registration period (1)

5 (a) One mark for each point to a maximum of two marks.
- A system that is used by senior managers (1)
- To supply them with information (1)
- In order to help them with their decision making (1)

(b) One mark to a maximum of two marks for each point about an appropriate task.
Example answer:
The head might use information about intakes in the primary feeder schools in order to produce long-term plans (1) for resources such as rooms, equipment and staff (1)

Worksheet 1: Organizations: school, home and environment anagrams

▶ **TEACHER'S RESOURCE GUIDE TOPIC 5 PAGE 35**

1 Optical mark recognition
2 Smart card
3 Swipe card
4 Biometric
5 Logging
6 Fingerprinting
7 Retinal
8 Magnetic
9 Management
10 Logging rate

Worksheet 2: Computers in control?

▶ **TEACHER'S RESOURCE GUIDE TOPIC 5 PAGE 36**

Place where you might find computers in control	Example 2	Example 3
In your school	Burglar alarm system	Automatic watering system for the school playing fields
In your home	DVD recorder	Central heating system
At a fairground/ theme park	Metal detection system for security	To control the operation of a camera on a ride
Along a road	Traffic light control system	Barrier system to control the entry to a car park
In a shopping centre	Controlling the sprinkler system in case of fire	Controlling the heating/air conditioning

Worksheet 3: Describing how control is used

▶ **TEACHER'S RESOURCE GUIDE TOPIC 5 PAGE 37**

Place where you might find computers in control	Example	How control is used
In your home	Washing machine	To allow the right amount of water to enter. To heat the water up to a certain temperature, add the powder and wash for a certain time. To drain water and add more to rinse and then to empty the water and heat washing till it is dry.
At a fairground/ theme park	To count people passing through the turnstiles	To activate a counter each time the turnstile moves enough to allow a person to enter.
Along a road	Fog warning system	Light sensors will come on when there is fog obstructing the area between the light source and the light cell. When the sensor detects fog, the warning signs light up. When the fog clears, the warning signs are turned off automatically.
In a shopping centre	Controlling the barrier in the car park	When car approaches, a ticket is printed and on its removal, the barrier rises. The car is detected having passed the barrier and the barrier is instructed to close.

Multiple-choice questions

▶ **TEACHER'S RESOURCE GUIDE TOPIC 5 PAGE 40**

1B, 2A, 3A, 4A, 5C, 6B, 7A, 8D, 9C, 10B

▶ Worksheet pp. 68–73

ICT and learning anagrams

Here are some words or phrases that have been jumbled up. The words are connected with ICT and learning. Can you work out what they are? There is a clue to help you.

1 Scan trot   *Hint: Determines the difference between the light and dark parts of the screen.*

Answer: _____

2 Love mu   *Hint: You can turn it up.*

Answer: _____

3 Phenol screen   *Hint: The help you get on the computer.*

Answer: _____

4 Control plane   *Hint: Where you change the settings using Windows.*

Answer: _____

5 Ironstone recluse   *Hint: Measure of the number of pixels on the screen.*

Answer: _____

6 Trust cosh   *Hint: Quick ways of accessing programs.*

Answer: _____

7 Tile aid mum   *Hint: Lots of different types of media.*

Answer: _____

8 Cent not   *Hint: The material such as text and graphics.*

Answer: _____

9 Liberal   *Hint: Raised dots used by visually impaired people.*

Answer: _____

10 Cipher moon   *Hint: What you speak into.*

Answer: _____

▶ **Activity**   p. 73

Voice recognition software

A company called Nuance makes a very popular piece of voice recognition software called Naturally Speaking.

Access the following website: http://www.nuance.com/naturallyspeaking/

You will notice that there are some things to try on this site.

Try the following:
- Typing challenge – where you have to see if you can beat someone using voice recognition software by typing in a piece of text.
- Turning talk into text – which is a nice demonstration of voice recognition software.

You are also free to find out more about the software.

See if you can find out about the following:
- Typical applications of how voice recognition software can be used.
- The hardware needed for voice recognition.
- Typical speeds compared to typing.
- How much the software costs.

▶ Multiple-choice questions

pp. 68–73

1 It is possible to adjust the contrast on a computer screen. Contrast means which of the following?

A The difference between the dark and light parts of the screen

B How many dots of light are displayed on the screen

C How large the screen is

D How long it takes to display an image on the screen

2 Users are able to alter the desktop environment when they use a computer. Which one of the following is *not* part of the desktop environment that can be adjusted?

A Icon size

B Screen resolution

C Window size

D Size of computer screen

3 Which one of the following statements about screen resolution is incorrect?

A It determines the number of pixels on the screen

B It will determine the size of a photograph on the screen

C The greater the screen resolution, the greater the number of pixels on the screen

D You cannot adjust screen resolution

4 Which one of the following concerning Windows in a GUI is incorrect?

A You cannot adjust the size of a window

B Windows can be maximized

C Windows can be minimized

D Windows can be displayed over other windows

5 Print settings are used to adjust which one of these?

A Which printer is used as the default printer

B What document is printed

C The content of the document

D The amount of paper in the paper tray

6 The main reason for organizing files in folders is which one of these?

A So they can easily be found when needed

B So the file can take less space when stored

C Because they look better in coloured folders

D Because folders cannot be copied

7 Which one of the following statements about icon size is incorrect?

A Icon size can depend on the screen resolution

B Larger icons are suitable for young children

C Icon size can be adjusted in the desktop environment

D Icon size can be altered by adjusting the font size

8 On-screen help is which one of these?

A A printed instruction book

B The help section in a computer magazine

C Help that appears in a window when you are using the computer and require help

D Telephone support when you ring a help centre

pp. 68–73

▶ Multiple-choice questions
(continued)

9 One feature of the desktop environment is password protection.

Password protection is which one of these?

A A password which everyone knows
B A password only you know that is needed to access a computer
C A virus checker
D A firewall

10 **Which one of the following are you least likely to find as part of a control panel?**

A Display settings
B Security settings
C Internet connectivity settings
D Database software

ANSWERS

Questions A

▶ TEXTBOOK PAGE 71

1 One mark for each feature to a maximum of three marks such as:
- Use ICT to teach a subject or topic
- Content – to instruct students in the subject
- Simulations – to help students understand complex situations
- Animations – to help students understand how things work
- Drill and practice – to help students consolidate the learning
- Tests – to let students know how well they have learnt the topic
- Games – to introduce fun into the learning process
- Learning can be done at a distance (i.e. away from the school/college premises)

2 (a) One mark for each point to a maximum of two marks similar to the following:
- Assessment that is taken on a computer or online (1) that is marked automatically by the computer (1)

(b) One mark for an advantage such as:
- The results are obtained immediately
- Can analyse what you did well on and what you did less well on so you can target your revision
- Frees up teacher time as there are no assessments to mark

One mark for a disadvantage such as:
- Danger of hackers accessing the system and changing marks
- Reliance on equipment that may go wrong
- Only suitable for certain types of assessment, as it would be hard to get a computer to mark an essay

3 (a) One mark for virtual learning environment.

(b) Two marks for a definition similar to the following:
- A virtual learning environment (VLE) is a software system (1) that uses the Internet to support teaching and learning in a school, college or other educational institution (1)

Two marks (one mark each) for two advantages such as:
- Students can access the VLE using any computer or portable device that will connect to the Internet
- Learning can take place at any time – the student is not restricted to learning only in lessons
- Students can assess themselves at any time – this makes them feel more responsible for their own learning and progress
- Can individualize learning – students can do work that is more closely matched to their ability. They do not have to wait for others to catch up with them

(c) One mark each for two disadvantages such as:
- The software is very expensive
- There is a danger of hackers altering reports, test marks, etc.
- Staff need a lot of training to use them
- Entering content can be time consuming

Questions B

▶ TEXTBOOK PAGE 73

1 (a) Two advantages (one mark each) such as:
- Reduces the risk of contracting RSI
- Can speak faster than typing, so it saves time
- Can increase productivity as more work can be achieved in the same time
- Provides a good interface for users with poor keyboarding skills
- Can do work away from the computer using a wireless microphone
- Saves money because you do not need to pay someone to take dictation and then type up

(b) Any two (one mark each) such as:
- Can use the system to issue commands to the operating system such as copy, delete, etc.
- Can dictate emails rather than type them
- Can dictate letters straight into the word-processing software

(c) Two reasons (one mark each) such as:
- Unusual or technical words may be unknown to the system
- System may not be able to understand certain accents
- Background noise such as phones ringing or other people talking may confuse the system
- The system may not be familiar with a new user's voice

2 One mark for an advantage such as:
- No keyboarding skills are needed to access the system
- Easy interface to use as you simply touch on items on the screen
- Easy to use a touch screen standing up – using a keyboard standing up is much more difficult

Case study: A touch screen making use of Braille

▶ TEXTBOOK PAGE 73

1 (a) One mark for one device such as:
- Mobile phone
- Tablet PC
- Information kiosk/point
- POS/till in a restaurant
- Control for a device such as central heating, speakers, etc.

(b) One mark for:
- Very little training needed
- Screen area that you touch/buttons on screen can be made large
- People with poor coordination skills/eyesight can use the screen

2 One mark for each point to a maximum of three marks:
- Areas of the screen vibrate
- High frequency for dots and low frequency for absent dots
- Used to represent Braille
- Blind or partially sighted person can read the Braille on the screen

Test yourself

▶ TEXTBOOK PAGE 74

A desktop environment
B control panel
C folders
D Shortcuts

E   password
F   Online assessment
G   VLE
H   Voice recognition
I   Text to voice

Examination style questions

▶ **TEXTBOOK PAGE 74**

1   (a)   One mark for microphone (also accept Bluetooth headset)
    (b)   One mark for screen/printer/Braille printer
    (c)   One mark for each point to a maximum of three marks.
          • You speak into a microphone
          • The voice pattern is compared with stored voice patterns
          • A match is found and the word is displayed on the screen
          • Or a command is recognized and issued to the operating system
          • The text can be proof read and mistakes corrected

2   (a)   One mark each for two features to a maximum of two marks.
          • They allow student performance to be assessed using tests and assessments that are marked automatically by the computer
          • They allow teachers to upload content – they can put their notes, presentations, videos, etc., on the VLE so students can access them
          • Communication – they allow students to communicate with each other and also with their teachers
          • They allow students to submit their work electronically – projects, essays, assignments, etc., can be submitted to the teachers
          • They allow teachers to return marked student work
          • They allow peer assessment – this means that the students mark each other's work
          • They can set up blogs – this allows students to discuss their work with each other and offer help to each other
          • Homework can be set and tailored more to an individual's ability
    (b)   One mark each for two advantages to a maximum of two marks.
          • Students can access the VLE using any computer or portable device that will connect to the Internet
          • Learning can take place at any time – the student is not restricted to learning only in lessons
          • Students can assess themselves at any time – this makes them feel more responsible for their own learning and progress
          • Can individualize learning – students can do work that is more closely matched to their ability. They do not have to wait for others to catch up with them

3   (a)   One mark for a meaning such as:
          • You can adjust the settings of the operating system (1)
          • Make adjustments to suit the way that you work or your own personal preferences (1)
          One mark for each example up to two marks such as:
          • Change screen settings (e.g., brightness, contrast, screen resolution)
          • Change colour schemes
          • Change mouse settings (e.g., speed you need to double click)
          • Change desktop fonts
          • Change icon size
    (b)   Two examples (one mark each) such as:
          • Alter the size of icons
          • Increase the size of desktop fonts
          • Use speech/voice recognition rather than the keyboard
          • Use a large keyboard on the screen that can be used with a mouse or joystick
          • Use text to voice settings so the system can read out words they have typed
          • Use a Braille keyboard

Worksheet: ICT and learning anagrams

▶ **TEACHER'S RESOURCE GUIDE TOPIC 6 PAGE 46**

1 Contrast
2 Volume
3 On screen help
4 Control panel
5 Screen resolution
6 Shortcuts
7 Multimedia
8 Content
9 Braille
10 Microphone

Multiple-choice questions

▶ **TEACHER'S RESOURCE GUIDE TOPIC 6 PAGE 48**

1A, 2D, 3D, 4A, 5A, 6A, 7D, 8C, 9B, 10D

▶ Worksheet 1   pp. 80–81

Applications software anagrams

Here are some words or phrases that have been jumbled up. The words are connected with Applications software. Can you work out what they are? There is a clue to help you.

1 Desert phase   *Hint: Software good for manipulating numerical data.*

Answer: _____

2 Progress cod win   *Hint: Software you would write a letter with.*

Answer: _____

3 Ship build kept song   *Hint: Software good for combing text and graphics.*

Answer: _____

4 Patient snore   *Hint: Software used to present material on slides.*

Answer: _____

5 Plastic piano   *Hint: Type of software used to do a specific job.*

Answer: _____

6 Generosity stamp   *Hint: Software that controls the hardware directly.*

Answer: _____

7 Romp rag   *Hint: Step-by-step instructions.*

Answer: _____

8 A bad seat   *Hint: Software that puts data into a certain structure.*

Answer: _____

9 Woodland   *Hint: Obtaining software using the Internet.*

Answer: _____

10 Ray poll   *Hint: Program used for working out wages.*

Answer: _____

▶ Worksheet 2

pp. 80–81

The best software for the job

Applications software does a particular job or application. On this course you will be using a variety of different software.

For this activity you have to produce a list of typical applications for which the software can be used. To give you the idea, the first one about word-processing software has been done for you. If you get stuck, use the Internet and the Student Book to help you with the answers.

Word-processing software

Writing letters
Producing short documents
Writing CVs
Sending personalized letters to lots of different people by performing a mail merge
Writing a report
Producing a simple invoice
Etc.

Spreadsheet software

_____

_____

_____

_____

_____

_____

_____

_____

Database software

_____

_____

_____

_____

_____

_____

_____

Website design software

_____

_____

_____

_____

_____

Desktop publishing (DTP) software

_____

_____

_____

_____

_____

_____

▶ Multiple-choice questions

pp. 80–81

1 Which one of the following is an example of applications software?

A Windows Vista
B Mac OS
C Linux
D Word-processing software

2 Which of the following is software used to perform a specific task such as complete a payroll?

A Virus checking software
B Applications software
C Operating systems software
D File management software

3 Which one of the following is *not* a type of applications software?

A Payroll package
B Word-processing package
C Spreadsheet package
D Operating systems software

4 Presentation software is an example of which of the following?

A Application software
B Operating systems software
C Database software
D Virus checking software

5 Which one of the following is an example of software?

A Hard disk
B CD-ROM
C Word-processing
D DVD drive

6 Which one of the following is an example of an applications package?

A The operating system
B Word-processing software
C A network operating system
D A hard disk

7 Which one of these is an advantage in getting someone to write software for a company instead of using a mass produced package?

A It is cheaper
B It does not take as long
C The company will get software that fits their needs perfectly
D It saves having to wait

8 Which one of the following is *not* performed by an operating system?

A Allocating space for files on a disk
B Issuing an instruction to the printer to start printing
C Managing the flow of data from the keyboard
D Searching for a record in a database

9 Using the Windows operating system, you can print out a large amount of material while you are doing some word-processing. This is called which of these?

A Transaction processing
B Batch processing
C Multitasking
D Spellchecking

10 How many pieces of applications software are shown in the list below?

Payroll
Database
Word-processing
Windows Vista

A 1
B 2
C 3
D 4

ANSWERS

Questions A

▶ **TEXTBOOK PAGE 81**

1 (a) One mark for each point to a maximum of two marks.
   - Step-by-step instructions (1)
   - That tells the computer what to do (1)
   - Written in a certain programming language (1)
   (b) One mark each for the two answers:
   - Operating systems software/systems software
   - Applications software
   - Note do not accept brand names such as Windows, Word, etc.
2 (a) One mark for each point to a maximum of two marks.
   - Applications software is software or program instructions (1) that are capable of doing a specific job (1)
   (b) One mark for each of three sources such as:
   - Files on disks
   - Files on removable media such as pen drives/flash drives/memory sticks
   - CD-ROMs or DVDs
   - Databases
   - The Internet
3 (a) One mark for 'Internet'
   (b) One mark for 'Databases'

Test yourself

▶ **TEXTBOOK PAGE 82**

A Internet
B files/DVDs
C database
D program
E operating system
F applications software
G word-processing, payroll

Examination style questions

▶ **TEXTBOOK PAGE 82**

1 One mark each (four marks total)
   Task 1 Word-processing
   Task 2 Desktop publishing
   Task 3 Spreadsheet
   Task 4 Database
2 One mark each for:
   - Underlining text in a word-processing program
   - Adding up columns of numbers
   - Adjusting the size of an image taken using a digital camera
3 One mark for the source and one mark for a brief description of the type of information × 3.
   - Files on disks (1) – pre-installed packages containing clip art, photographs, borders, templates (1)
   - File on flash drives/memory sticks (1), etc., – files you wish to transfer between computers such as essays and coursework (1)
   - CD-ROMs and DVDs (1) – used for encyclopaedias that can be used for reference and content (1)
   - The Internet – used for images/pictures (1), used to cut and paste text (1), etc.

Worksheet 1: Applications software anagrams

▶ **TEACHER'S RESOURCE GUIDE TOPIC 7 PAGE 52**

1 Spreadsheet
2 Word processing
3 Desktop publishing
4 Presentation
5 Applications
6 Operating system
7 Program
8 Database
9 Download
10 Payroll

Multiple-choice questions

▶ **TEACHER'S RESOURCE GUIDE TOPIC 7 PAGE 55**

1D, 2B, 3D, 4A, 5C, 6B, 7C, 8D, 9C, 10C

▶ Worksheet 1   pp. 88–89

Search criteria

Task 1: What do these search criteria do?

Here are some search criteria used in queries. Explain in simple terms what each one does.

1   =2010 (in a date field)
2   <=12/02/09 (in a date field)
3   ="Jones" (in a text field for a surname)
4   >=45 (in a number field for quantity)
5   <>0 (in a number field for quantity)
6   <0 (in a currency field for account balance)
7   >31/12/07 AND <01/01/09 (in a date field)

Task 2: Creating search criteria

Now you have to create the search criteria from the description given.

1   The date equal to 01/01/10
2   A date before the date 03/05/99
3   A date equal to or after the date 1999
4   A date between but not including the dates 07/09/87 and 06/09/90
5   A number greater than 20
6   A number less than or equal to 45
7   A number that is not equal to zero
8   A currency that is not negative

▶ Worksheet 2   pp. 88–95

Information handling software anagrams

Here are some words or phrases that have been jumbled up. The words are connected with Information handling software. Can you work out what they are? There is a clue to help you.

1 Paint dug   *Hint: Process of keeping information up to date.*

Answer: _____

2 Glide net   *Hint: Removing old information.*

Answer: _____

3 Storing   *Hint: Putting data into ascending or descending order.*

Answer: _____

4 Change sir   *Hint: Looking for information.*

Answer: _____

5 Ear troop   *Hint: Less than.*

Answer: _____

6 Ale boon   *Hint: Data type where there are two alternatives.*

Answer: _____

7 Cod err   *Hint: Part of a file.*

Answer: _____

8 Filed   *Hint: Part of a file*

Answer: _____

9 Bleat   *Hint: Something you organize data in.*

Answer: _____

10 Encasing here   *Hint: Something you use to find information off the Internet.*

Answer: _____

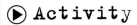

▶ Activity   pp. 94–95

Creating passwords

People do not always take creating passwords seriously enough and this can compromise the security of (personal) information held on systems.

For this activity you have to use the Internet and the Student Book to learn about creating good passwords and rules about how to look after them.

Once you have completed your research, you have to produce a poster with the aim of alerting users about the problems and a series of rules about passwords that will help keep the information more secure.

▶ Multiple-choice questions

pp. 88–95

1 **Place the following parts to a database in order of size with the largest first.**

   A File, Field, Record
   B File, Record, Field
   C Field, Record, File
   D Record, Field, File

2 **What is the main reason for *not* using the surname of a person as the key field in a large database?**

   A Surnames can be long so there will be too much typing
   B More than one person could have the same surname
   C Surnames can be hard to spell
   D For security reasons

3 **Here is a table showing details of customers and the orders they have placed:**

Customer No	Customer Name	Order No	Order Date	Order Value
1211	K. Jones	19870	12/12/10	£500
1365	F. Smith	18762	14/12/10	£1900
1201	J. Simpson	21101	22/12/10	£231

   Which one of the following statements is true?

   A There is only one key field used
   B There are two key fields used
   C There are no key fields used
   D There are five key fields used

4 **The data in a database can be brought up-to-date. Which one of these processes would *not* be classed as updating?**

   A Deleting
   B Amending
   C Inserting
   D Sorting

5 **To find specific information from a database you would need to perform which of the following?**

   A A query
   B A print
   C A sort
   D A validation

6 **When data is put into a database it is checked to make sure that the data is in the correct format for the field. What is this called?**

   A Validation
   B Verification
   C Searching
   D Lookup

7 **Which one of the following is *not* a data type?**

   A Number
   B Text
   C Date
   D Weather

8 Here is a set of numbers: 1, 8, 5, 12, 3, 9, 2

When sorted into descending order, the first number in the list would be which one of the following?

A   12
B   1
C   5
D   2

9 A key field is which one of the following?

A   A password
B   A field in a database used to identify a record
C   Any field in a database
D   A date field

---

10 =, <>, <, >, are examples of which one of the following?

A   Operators
B   Functions
C   Types of data
D   Fields

ANSWERS

Questions A

▶ **TEXTBOOK PAGE 89**

1 One mark for the definition and one mark for the example similar to the following:
Updating means bringing data up-to-date owing to changes that may have occurred since the data was originally input (1). For example, a person could have changed their address (1).

2 One mark for each point to a maximum of two marks:
- Searching means locating specific information (1)
- Sorting means putting all the data into a certain order (1)

3 One mark for each of the following:
- Ascending order – in alphabetical order with As first, then Bs and so on
- Descending order – in order with the Zs first and the As last

Questions B

▶ **TEXTBOOK PAGE 91**

1 (a) One mark each for two from: Reg-number, Make, Model or Year
  (b) One mark for Reg-number
  (c) One mark for an explanation such as:
    - It is the only field that is unique
    - No two registration numbers are the same
  (d) One mark for a 'record'
  (e) One mark for seven

2 (a) One mark for each sensible field name up to a maximum of four marks such as:
    - Surname
    - Initial
    - Address/First line address
    - Postcode
    - Telephone number
  (b) (i) One mark for any answer similar to the following:
      - Key field has to be unique
      - Surname is not unique as there are two people with the same surname
    (ii) One mark for one of the following:
      - Employee ID
      - Employee No
      - Etc.
    (iii) One mark for AutoNumber

Questions C

▶ **TEXTBOOK PAGE 93**

1 (a) One mark for each point to a maximum of two marks.
    A check performed by the computer/information handling software (1) to make sure that the data is allowable (1).
  (b) One mark for each validation check to a maximum of two marks.
    - Range check
    - Data type check
    - Presence check
    - Format check
    - Check digit

2 (a) One mark for each point similar to the following to a maximum of two marks.

Reports are used to present the output (1) from an information handling system usually as a printout on paper (1).

  (b) One mark for each item such as:
    - Title
    - Date
    - Page numbers
    - Details of who produced the report

Questions D

▶ **TEXTBOOK PAGE 95**

1 (a) One mark for a definition such as:
    A series of characters that are entered by a user to verify that they are who they say they are when accessing information.
  (b) One mark for each point to a maximum of two marks:
    - Passwords should not be disclosed to others
    - Users should not log on using another person's password
    - Passwords should be long and consist of numbers and letters
    - Passwords should never be written down
    - Passwords should be changed regularly
  (c) One mark for each point to a maximum of two marks:
    - Allow certain staff to access only certain files
    - Only allow staff to access those files needed for their job
    - Determine what you can do with the data in the files
    - For example, read only, read/write, delete, etc.

2 (a) One mark for a definition such as:
    The correctness of the data stored
  (b) One mark for each point to a maximum of two marks such as:
    - Ensure that errors are not introduced when data is input into the system by using verification techniques
    - Use validation checks
    - Ensure that the data is updated regularly
    - Ensure that data no longer needed is deleted

Test yourself

▶ **TEXTBOOK PAGE 96**

A Updating
B sorted
C Searching, criteria
D operators
E key field
F record
G fields
H file
I validation

Examination style questions

▶ **TEXTBOOK PAGE 97**

1 (a) One mark for a total of three correct fields:
    (i) Text (Characters)
    (ii) Text (Characters)
    (iii) Boolean/Logical
  (b) Three fields (one mark each) such as:
    - Form teacher
    - Form

- Date of entry into school
- Exam results
- Number of half days in school
- Pupil email address
- Pupil mobile number
- Name of parent/guardian
- Parent/guardian work telephone number
- Medical problems
- Medication taken

(c) One mark for the name of the field and one mark for an explanation.
UniquePupilNumber – as no two pupils can have the same number, so it is used to identify pupils who could have the same names

(d) One mark each for two errors such as:
- Transcription errors – where data copied from forms is misread
- Transposition errors – where digits are incorrectly reversed when being typed into the database

(e) One mark for each method that is applicable to the answer in part (d) × 2.
- Verification where after the data is keyed in it is proof read against the original document used to supply the information such as an application form
- Validation checks such as a check digit added to the unique pupil number which checks that all the other numbers in the pupil number have been input correctly

2 One mark for each difference similar to the following:
Search is used to find specific information (1) whereas a sort puts the information into a certain order (1)

3 One mark for a statement of the 'how' with an example for the second mark.
It is easier to take backup copies (1). With a manual system copies would need to be taken using a photocopier (1)

4 (a) One mark for each of the following key fields:
Customer number and Item code

(b) One mark for Delivery

(c) One mark each for two sensible fields such as:
Date of order, Description of item, Qty ordered, VAT, etc.

(d) One mark for the name of the validation check and one mark for a brief description of its use. For example:
Use a list where the user is presented with a list of sizes such as Large, Medium or Small (1). They have to select one of these to proceed so this limits the data (1).

(e) One mark for 4

(f) One mark each for two correct entries.

Fieldname	Operator	Search criteria
Size	=	Small

AND

Fieldname	Operator	Search criteria
Delivery	=	Y

Worksheet 1: Search criteria

▶ **TEACHER'S RESOURCE GUIDE TOPIC 8 PAGE 57**

Task 1: What do these search criteria do?

1 Lists the data where the date has the year of 2010
2 Lists the data where the date is equal to or before the date 12/02/09
3 Lists the data where the surname is Jones
4 Lists the data where the quantity is greater than or equal to 45
5 Lists the data where the quantity is not zero
6 Lists the data where the account balance is less than zero (i.e. negative)
7 Lists the data where the date is after 31/12/07 and before 01/01/09

Task 2: Creating search criteria

1 = 2010
2 <=03/05/99
3 >=1999
4 >07/09/87 AND <06/09/90
5 >20
6 <=45
7 <>0
8 >=0

Worksheet 2: Information handling software anagrams

▶ **TEACHER'S RESOURCE GUIDE TOPIC 8 PAGE 58**

1 Updating
2 Deleting
3 Sorting
4 Searching
5 Operator
6 Boolean
7 Record
8 Field
9 Table
10 Search engine

Multiple-choice questions

▶ **TEACHER'S RESOURCE GUIDE TOPIC 8 PAGE 60**

1B, 2B, 3B, 4D, 5A, 6A, 7D, 8A, 9B, 10A

▶ Worksheet

pp. 102–106

Email anagrams

Here are some words or phrases that have been jumbled up. The words are connected with Email. Can you work out what they are? There is a clue to help you.

1 A mile   *Hint: An electronic message.*

Answer: _____

2 Pug or   *Hint: You can send email to this.*

Answer: _____

3 Fanatic them let   *Hint: A file sent with an email.*

Answer: _____

4 Far word   *Hint: An email sent to you that you send on to others.*

Answer: _____

5 Basked doors   *Hint: Where you keep your list of contact email addresses.*

Answer: _____

6 A vibe us   *Hint: You must not use this kind of language in emails.*

Answer: _____

7 Crab copy on   *Hint: Copy of an email sent to others for their information.*

Answer: _____

8 Crop ninety   *Hint: Method of keeping emails private.*

Answer: _____

9 Maps   *Hint: Unwanted email that you waste time deleting.*

Answer: _____

10 Versus I   *Hint: Emails are checked for these by your virus checker.*

Answer: _____

▶ Activity 1 | pp. 102–104

Practise sending email

Take a look at the email facility that you are familiar with.

1 Set up an address book with the names and email addresses of at least ten of your friends or relatives. Use this address book to send an email to one of your friends.

2 Explain briefly what an address book is and how it can be useful to someone who uses email.

3 Set up a mailing list (group) to send the same email message to at least four of your friends. After you have learnt how to do this, write a list explaining the steps you took so that you can refer to this in the future.

4 Explain briefly what a mailing list (group) is and how it is useful to someone who uses email.

5 Set up a file to send with an email. This file could be a word-processed document, a spreadsheet, an image. Attach the file to an email and send it to one of your friends. Send an email message with the file to tell them that you have sent them a file and what it consists of.

6 Explain the steps involved in attaching a file to an email.

▶ Activity 2 | pp. 102–104

Explaining the features of email

For this activity you have to explain some of the features of email using a screen shot.

A screen shot is a picture of the screen you are looking at.

To perform a screen shot of the screen you are looking at you press down the Ctrl key and keeping it pressed down then click the Prt Scr key.

A copy of the entire screen is held in the clipboard and this allows you to paste it into a document like this.

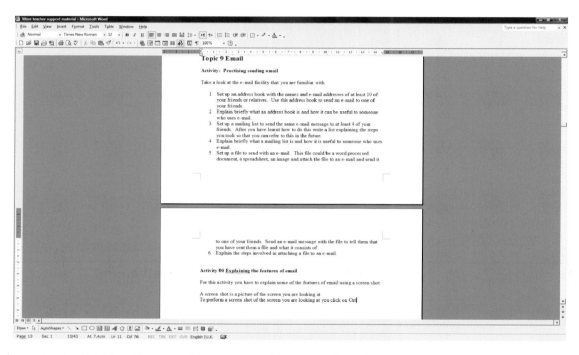

You have to do this for the opening screen of the email package you use.

You now have to paste this into a word-processed document. When you have done this, you need to explain the various parts/features of the email package by making use of arrows and text boxes. This process is called annotation.

When you have completed this work, save a copy and print the work out to show to your teacher/lecturer.

▶ Multiple-choice questions | pp. 102–106

1 Which of the following is *not* an advantage of email?

A It is less formal than a letter and so takes less time to write

B You do not need a stamp and an envelope

C It is easy to send the same email to several people

D Everyone can be contacted using email

2 Which one of the following is a disadvantage of email compared with ordinary post?

A You cannot contact everyone as not everyone has email facilities

B You can send email from your own home, no need to go to the post box

C Email is cheaper than a letter (no paper, no envelope and no stamp to buy)

D Email can be sent and received on many mobile phones

3 The abbreviation cc stands for which one of these?

A Circulation copy

B Carbon copy

C Cancellation copy

D Copy copy

4 The abbreviation bcc stands for which one of these?

A Blind carbon copy

B Backup carbon copy

C Blinkered carbon copy

D Bound carbon copy

5 Which one of these is a disadvantage of sending personal data using email?

A You cannot read it

B It may be intercepted and read

C It is illegal to send personal information using a computer

D It is faster than ordinary mail

6 Which one of the following is an advantage in using email?

A Emails arrive faster

B Emails are more secure than posted documents

C Emails are more expensive to send than posted documents

D Emails are always printed out

7 Which one of the following would you *not* normally find in an email signature?

A Name

B Address

C Phone number

D The email address of the person you are sending the email to

8 What is an email group?

A A list of people and their email addresses

B A file attachment

C A list of everyone to whom you are likely to send email

D A type of browser

9 What is an address book?

A A list of people and their email addresses

B A file attachment

C A list of everyone to whom you are likely to send email

D A type of browser

10 Why should you *not* open an attachment to an email from a person who you do not know?

A It might not work

B You cannot attach files to emails

C It could contain a virus

D It could take a long time to load

ANSWERS

Questions A

▶ **TEXTBOOK PAGE 104**

1 (a) One mark for each point to a maximum of two marks.
- An email is an electronic message (1) sent from one communication device (computer, telephone, mobile phone, or portable digital assistant) to another (1)

(b) Two marks for two points in the definition and one mark for a suitable example such as:
- A copy of the original email (1) which was sent to a person in the main email address and circulated to all those people in the list of email addresses in the cc box (1)
- A carbon copy is sent to everyone else who needs to see a copy of the original email (1)
- A teacher can send a copy of an email about bad behaviour to a student and then carbon copy (cc) other people in such as the year head, the deputy head, etc. (1)

(c) Two marks for two points in the definition and one mark for a suitable example such as:
- Groups are lists of people and their email addresses (1). They are used when a copy of email needs to be distributed to people in a particular group (1)
- For example, a teacher could remind a group of GCSE ICT students that their coursework needs to be handed in the following week. The same email is sent the once but appears in all those students' email boxes (1)

2 (a) One mark for an answer such as:
- Enables a recipient's email address to be selected by clicking on it rather than typing it in (1)
- Saves time because you do not need to enter the email address using a keyboard (1)

(b) One mark for an answer such as:
- Can put people who need to get the same email into a group (1)
- You only need to send the one email and everyone in the group will receive it (1)

(c) One mark for an answer such as:
- Can attach images, word-processed documents, spreadsheet files and send them with the email (1)
- Can send one or more files with an email (1)

Questions B

▶ **TEXTBOOK PAGE 106**

1 (a) One mark for each advantage up to two marks.
- You can attach files and send them with the email
- They are stored on the computer, so there are no paper files to store
- Emails are almost free to send
- The same email can be sent to a group of people

(b) One mark for each disadvantage up to two marks.
- Emails with attachments can contain viruses
- Spam email takes up time because it needs to be deleted
- Not everybody has an email account

2 One mark for each misuse × 2.
- Virus attack
- Cyberbullying
- Inappropriate language
- Hacking
- Identity theft
- Spam
- Paedophiles grooming young children

One mark for each method of prevention × 2.
Ensure that the prevention is appropriate to the misuse
- Virus attack – ensure that emails with attachments are not opened unless you know who they are from
- Cyber bullying – the network manager should use software that checks incoming and outgoing emails for certain words/phrases that would indicate bullying, so action can be taken
- Inappropriate language – people should realize that abusive and threatening language has no place in communication on the Internet so any emails containing such language are sent to the network manager/ISP to deal with
- Hacking – use a firewall to prevent illegal access using the Internet
- Identity theft – do not reply to emails asking for banking details
- Spam – use a spam filter
- Paedophiles grooming young children – parents should set up parental control to ensure their children are not able to freely access chat rooms, message boards, etc.

Test yourself

▶ **TEXTBOOK PAGE 107**

A address
B signature
C address
D forward
E cc
F bcc
G attachment
H encrypted
I monitoring
J spam

Examination style questions

▶ **TEXTBOOK PAGE 107**

1 (a) One mark for each point to a maximum of two marks similar to the following:
- An electronic message (1) sent between computers networked together (1)

(b) One mark for one of the following:
- It is almost instantaneous (1)
- There is no chance of losing it (1)
- There is no storage required (1)
- The student has a backup copy (1)
- They do not need to find the teacher (1)
- The teacher can mark the work and return it by email (1)

(c) One mark for an answer similar to:
- It is a file which is sent with an email (1)

(d) One mark for an answer similar to:
- It reduces the file size and this means that it will be sent faster

2 (a) One mark for the factor and one mark for the advantage it gives × 3.
Suitable answers such as:
- Faster as the same email message can be sent to lots of different staff

- Cheaper as there are no call costs especially if they use mobiles
- Can attach files – files can be attached and transferred instantly

(b) One mark for a brief description of the facility and one mark for way it makes it easier as a team × 2. Possible answers include:
  - Can form an email group so a single email can be sent to a whole group of people without having to type in all the email addresses in the circulation list
  - Use the reply facility – so an email sent from one of the staff can be replied to with the content of their original email present
  - Can attach files to emails – staff can transfer work they are working on with others for their comments

Worksheet: Email anagrams

▶ **TEACHER'S RESOURCE GUIDE TOPIC 9 PAGE 64**

1 Email
2 Group
3 File attachment
4 Forward
5 Address book
6 Abusive
7 Carbon copy
8 Encryption
9 Spam
10 Viruses

Multiple-choice questions

▶ **TEACHER'S RESOURCE GUIDE TOPIC 9 PAGE 67**

1D, 2A, 3B, 4A, 5B, 6A, 7D, 8A, 9C, 10C

▶ Worksheet   pp. 112–115

Spreadsheet software anagrams

Here are some words or phrases that have been jumbled up. The words are connected with Spreadsheet software. Can you work out what they are? There is a clue to help you.

1 All be   *Hint: Used for identifying a column of data.*

Answer: _____

2 Loaf rum   *Hint: A calculation in a spreadsheet.*

Answer: _____

3 Bales out   *Hint: A type of cell referencing.*

Answer: _____

4 Tear evil   *Hint: A type of cell referencing.*

Answer: _____

5 Gain ling   *Hint: Putting data in a certain position in a cell.*

Answer: _____

6 Rob red   *Hint: You can add this to a cell or group of cells.*

Answer: _____

7 Circulate loan   *Hint: The automatic calculation when cell contents change.*

Answer: _____

8 Rec cry nu   *Hint: A data type.*

Answer: _____

9 Fen potty   *Hint: Examples include Arial, Times New Roman, Courier etc.*

Answer: _____

10 Left stony   *Hint: Examples include bold, underline and italics.*

Answer: _____

▶ Multiple-choice questions | pp. 112–115

1 The following is typed into a spreadsheet cell: =b3*c3

This is which one of these?

A   A cell
B   A formula
C   A label
D   Data

2 Cell merging means which one of these?

A   Combining cells so that you can enter a long heading
B   Copying a formula down a column
C   Copying a formula across a row
D   Altering the margins

3 Labels are best described as which one of these?

A   Printouts of a spreadsheet
B   Text that identifies what a nearby cell/column/row represents
C   A formula
D   A function

4 Which one of the following is *not* classed as formatting?

A   Adding a border
B   Setting a range of cells to currency
C   Entering a formula
D   Changing the size of the font

5 Spreadsheets are often used by accountants. Which one of the following is *not* a benefit of using a spreadsheet?

A   Performing 'what if' investigations
B   Accurate calculation
C   Auto recalculation
D   The need for training to use one

6 =B6 is *not* which one of these?

A   A relative cell address
B   An absolute cell address
C   A formula
D   A formula that contains an absolute cell address

7 Which one of the following statements about a formula entered into a spreadsheet is incorrect?

A   Formulas always start with an equals sign
B   They contain one or more cell addresses
C   They can be copied
D   They are sometimes inaccurate

8 =AVERAGE(B1:B7) is a formula containing a function.

Which one of the following is incorrect?

A   The cell range is B1 to B7
B   AVERAGE is a function
C   It finds the mean of all the cells from B1 to B7
D   (B1:B7) is a function

9 Which one of the following is an advantage in using spreadsheets?

A   It is easy to generate graphs and charts automatically
B   Performing calculations manually
C   Totalling the numbers using a calculator
D   Writing totals on bits of paper

10 Which one of these is not a mathematical operator?

A   *
B   /
C   +
D $

ANSWERS

Questions A

▶ **TEXTBOOK PAGE 113**

1 (a) One mark for:
    A label is used for titles, headings, names, and for identifying columns or rows of data.
  (b) One mark for:
    Data are the values (text or numbers) that you enter into the spreadsheet.
  (c) One mark for:
    Formulas are used to perform calculations on the cell contents.

2 One mark each for Absolute and Relative

3 One mark each for two functions such as:
  • AVERAGE
  • SUM
  • COUNT
  • Etc.

Questions B

▶ **TEXTBOOK PAGE 115**

1 One mark for a correct tick.

Reason	Tick if reason is correct
If a cell changes, then all those cells that depend on the cell will change	√
A more accurate answer is produced than with a calculator	
It improves the appearance of the spreadsheet	
The formulas in the spreadsheet need to be kept secret	

2 One mark for each point to a maximum of two marks.
  • Change the font style
  • Change the font size
  • Change the colour of font
  • Use bold, underline, etc.
  • Use a background colour for the cell

Test yourself

▶ **TEXTBOOK PAGE 116**

A Data
B Labels
C Formulas
D specialist
E absolute
F relative
G absolute
H relative
I predictions
J recalculation

Examination style questions

▶ **TEXTBOOK PAGE 117**

1 (a) One mark for division
  (b) One mark for addition or add
  (c) One mark for multiplication
  (d) One mark for subtraction or minus

2 (a) One mark for Electricity
  (b) One mark for £15
  (c) One mark each for two correctly placed ticks.

Formula	Tick if formula gives correct total
=B2+B3+B4+B5+B6+B7+B8	
+A2+A3+A4+A5+A6+A7	
=sum(B2:B7)	√
=sum(A2:A7)	
=B2+B3+B4+B5+B6+B7	√

3 (a) One mark for: C =SUM(C2:F2)
  (b) One mark for =AVERAGE(G2:G12)
  (c) One mark for right justify/right align
  (d) One mark for 'cell merging'
  (e) One mark for each point to a maximum of two marks.
    • Automatic recalculation
    • Accurate calculations
    • Can perform 'what if' investigations
    • Can easily produce graphs and charts
    • It is easy to reuse the spreadsheet

Worksheet: Spreadsheet software anagrams

▶ **TEACHER'S RESOURCE GUIDE TOPIC 10 PAGE 70**

1 Label
2 Formula
3 Absolute
4 Relative
5 Aligning
6 Border
7 Recalculation
8 Currency
9 Font type
10 Font style

Multiple-choice questions

▶ **TEACHER'S RESOURCE GUIDE TOPIC 10 PAGE 71**

1B, 2A, 3B, 4C, 5D, 6A, 7D, 8D, 9A, 10D

▶ Activity 1   p. 123

Producing a template for a letter

A template for a letter saves time each time you produce a letter as it means that some of the content of the letter is already there.

Produce a template that can be used with word-processing software to help save time when writing a letter.

You should use the help facility of the software to help you if necessary.

Your template should include the following:
- a logo
- name and address and other contact details
- today's date (this should be entered automatically – you can use the online help to find out how you do this).

▶ Activity 2   p. 124

Choosing a font type

There are a huge number of font styles available and it is important to be able to choose the best font for a particular document.

Study the following font types (i.e., the font names and the shapes of the characters) and then answer the questions that follow.

Font 1   *Vladimir Script*

Font 2   Arial

Font 3   Times New Roman

Font 4   Verdana

Font 5   **Matura MT Script Capitals**

Font 6   Century Gothic

Which font would be best for each of these uses?

1   The text in a children's book to teach them to read.

2   The text to go on a map of Treasure Island to mark the landmarks.

3   Some text at the bottom of letter on a website to make it look as though the writer has signed it.

4   The text to go with an image of a witch on a Halloween poster.

5   A novel.

Creating diagrams using word-processing software

The following diagram has been created using word-processing software.

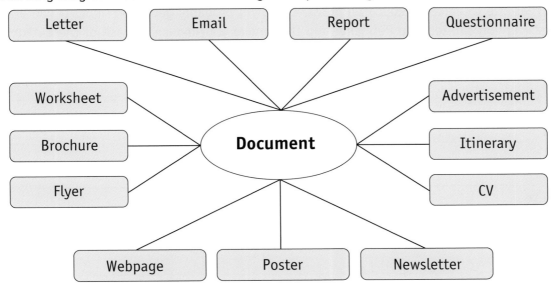

Load your word-processing package and by creating text boxes and lines create a diagram similar to the one show above.

Once you have created a diagram save it and print a copy out.

You are now going to improve the appearance of this diagram.

There are a number of ways you might do this and here are some suggestions:
- You can add colour to the diagram (e.g. font, lines etc.).
- You can add borders.
- You could put in some clip art.

When you have completed your final design save it, print it and give a copy to your teacher.

▶ **Activity 4** pp. 122–126

How much do you know about the DTP software Microsoft Publisher?

If you have used Microsoft Publisher before then you should know what each of these icons means. Feel free to make an educated guess – you will probably get them right. If you are totally stuck, you can load up Publisher and then move your mouse to each of the buttons where a label appears.

1 _____

2 _____

3 _____

4 _____

5 _____

6 _____

7 _____

8 _____

9 _____

10 _____

▶ Worksheet 1 | pp. 122–126

DTP software anagrams

Here are some words or phrases that have been jumbled up. The words are connected with DTP software. Can you work out what they are? There is a clue to help you.

1   A warm trek   *Hint: A feint picture used as a background.*

Answer: _____

2   Check sell rep   *Hint: Used to check spelling.*

Answer: _____

3   Assure hut   *Hint: Useful for ensuring that you use a variety of words in a sentence.*

Answer: _____

4   Bred or   *Hint: Lines or graphics put around the edge of a page or a box.*

Answer: _____

5   Email germ   *Hint: Combining a list of, say, names and addresses, with a standard letter.*

Answer: _____

6   Metal pet   *Hint: Use one of these so you don't have to worry about the design of a document.*

Answer: _____

7   Settles hey   *Hint: A document that sets out fonts and font sizes for headings and subheadings, etc., in a document.*

Answer: _____

8   Dare he   *Hint: Put at the top of the page.*

Answer: _____

9   Fore to   *Hint: Put at the bottom of the page.*

Answer: _____

10 Pasta house   *Hint: Shapes that are already stored by the software.*

Answer: _____

▶ Worksheet 2 | pp. 122–126

DTP: What do you already know?

You came across DTP as part of your Key Stage 3 study. How much can you remember? Try the following questions to find out.

1 What do the initials DTP stand for?

_____

2 (a) Give the names of three items of hardware other than the computer itself that would be useful for DTP.

Item 1: _____

Item 2: _____

Item 3: _____

(b) For each of the pieces of hardware you have listed in (a) say why it would be useful.

Item 1: _____

_____

Item 2: _____

_____

Item 3: _____

_____

3 Templates are often used in DTP. Explain what is meant by a template.

_____

_____

_____

4 Files from other software packages are often put into DTP documents.
Give two types of file that you could put into a DTP document.

File 1: _____

File 2: _____

▶ Multiple-choice questions | pp. 122–126

1 What does DTP stand for?

A Desktop publishing
B Desktop printing
C Desk to publisher
D Dump to printer

2 Which one of these hardware devices would *not* be useful when using DTP software?

A Digital camera
B Scanner
C Colour printer
D Magnetic ink character reader

3 Obtaining material from another file and incorporating this into a document in a DTP package is called which one of the following?

A Importing
B Exporting
C Emigrating
D Deleting

4 Which are the two formats for graphics files?

A Bitmap and vector
B Bitmap and clip art
C Vector and clip art
D CAD and CAM

5 A company wishes to produce its own company newsletter. The newsletter is to contain pictures, photographs, cartoons and text in a variety of different fonts. Which of the following would be the most appropriate software to use for this task?

A Desktop publishing
B Word-processing
C Presentation
D Spreadsheet

6 Spellcheckers are used to do which one of the following?

A To proof read a document
B To validate a document
C To check the spelling of words contained in a document
D To check the grammar in a document

7 Which one of the following is *not* an example of justifying text?

A Align right
B Align left
C Bold
D Centre

8 The word-processor checks all the words you have typed against an online dictionary. This is an example of which one of these?

A Grammar checking
B Mail merging
C Proof reading
D Spellchecking

9 Which of the following would you be least likely to put into a header or a footer?

A The company logo
B Today's date
C Date that the document was produced
D A page of text that explains the purpose of the document

10 To find words having similar meanings to a word typed in you could use which one of the following features?

A Mail merge
B Online thesaurus
C Table
D Border

ANSWERS

Questions A

▶ **TEXTBOOK PAGE 123**

1 (a) One mark for each point similar to the following to a maximum of two marks.
 • Compares the spelling of each word in a document (1).
 • Against a stored dictionary (1).
 • Highlights words spelt incorrectly (1).
 • Offers suggestions on how the word should be spelt (1).
 • Can correct spelling automatically (1).
 (b) One mark for one of the following:
 • Word may be spelt correctly but it could be the wrong word (e.g., too instead of two).
 • The grammar may be wrong.
 • The sentence may not make sense.
2 One mark for each point to a maximum of three marks.
 • Can use data already held for names and addresses.
 • Uses the one letter so you do not need to prepare different letters yourself.
 • Inserts the variable data automatically.
 • Can leave the computer to insert and print and do another task yourself.
3 One mark for each point to a maximum of two marks.
 • Can look for words with similar meaning (1).
 • By entering or highlighting a word and using the thesaurus (1).
 • For example, they might want to change the word 'important', which appears twice in a sentence, and the thesaurus would give them other choices such as 'vital' or 'significant' (1).

Questions B

▶ **TEXTBOOK PAGE 126**

1 (a) One mark for:
 Images that are already created and are stored that you can put in your documents.
 (b) One mark for:
 Taken from one place or software package and put into another software package.
 (c) One mark for each of the following to a maximum of two marks.
 • Provided with the software package you are using.
 • From libraries of clip art on CD.
 • From libraries of clip art on the Internet.
 • Using search engines such as Google to search for images.
 • Cutting and pasting from websites.
2 (a) One mark each for two of the following:
 • It can be resized (i.e., made bigger or smaller).
 • It can be rotated through a certain angle.
 • It can be mirror imaged (i.e., like reflecting the image in a mirror).
 • Part of the image can be cropped (this is just like cutting the part you want out of the picture).
 (b) One mark for each point to a maximum of two marks.
 A very feint image/graphic (1) used as a background to a document (1).
3 (a) One mark for an answer similar to:
 The shape of the characters (e.g., Arial, Times New Roman, Courier, etc.).

 (b) One mark for an answer similar to:
 The size of the set of characters.
 (c) One mark for an answer similar to:
 The use of formatting such as bold, underline and italics.

Test yourself

▶ **TEXTBOOK PAGE 127**

A documents
B thesaurus
C mail merge
D table
E Borders
F Double line
G resizing
H AutoShapes
I watermark

Examination style questions

▶ **TEXTBOOK PAGE 127**

1 (a) One mark for a similar answer to:
 • It is a letter that is individual to a particular person.
 • Letter makes reference to their name and address.
 • Letter contains information specific to them.
 (b) One mark for each point to a maximum of three marks.
 • Using ICT to send lots of individualized letters (1).
 • Makes use of a standard letter containing blanks (1).
 • The blanks are where the variable data from a name of and address file are inserted (1).
 • The computer performs the task automatically (1).
 (c) One mark for one advantage similar to the following:
 • Less time is spent producing the letters.
 • Data stored can be reused for other mail merges.
2 (a) One mark for Online thesaurus.
 (b) One mark for Spellchecker.
 (c) One mark for Mail merge.
3 One mark for each point to a maximum of six marks.
 • Copy and paste images off the Internet.
 • Create own images in a graphics or arts package and import them.
 • Draw diagrams in the DTP or word-processing package.
 • Scan an image in from a book.
 • Take a digital photograph and insert file into document.
 • Use the clip art available with the DTP package.
 • Import clip art from the Internet.
 • Use Google/search engine to look for image and then save the image and import into the document.
 • Use library of images on the Internet.
 • Scan old photographs in using a scanner.
 • Draw graphs and charts using a spreadsheet and then copy and paste.

Activity 2: Choosing a font type

▶ **TEACHER'S RESOURCE GUIDE TOPIC 11 PAGE 74**

1 The text in a children's book to teach them to read.
 Font 2   Arial
 Font 4   Verdana
2 The text to go on a map of Treasure Island to mark the landmarks.

font 5   _Matura MT Script Capitals_

3 Some text at the bottom of letter on a website to make it look as though the writer has signed it.

Font 1   _Vladimir Script_

4 The text to go with an image of a witch on a Halloween poster.

font 5   _Matura MT Script Capitals_

Font 6   Century Gothic

5 A novel

Font 3   Times New Roman

Activity 4: How much do you know about the DTP software Microsoft Publisher?

▶ **TEACHER'S RESOURCE GUIDE TOPIC 11 PAGE 76**

1 Columns
2 Justify (i.e. straight margins down each side)
3 Numbering (i.e. to create a numbered list)
4 Zoom out (i.e. make the page smaller)
5 Fill colour
6 Zoom in (i.e. make the page larger)
7 Rotate
8 Bring to front
9 Styles and formatting
10 Text box

Worksheet 1: DTP software anagrams

▶ **TEACHER'S RESOURCE GUIDE TOPIC 11 PAGE 77**

1 Watermark
2 Spellchecker
3 Thesaurus
4 Border
5 Mail merge
6 Template
7 Style sheet
8 Header
9 Footer
10 Autoshapes

Worksheet 2: DTP: What do you already know?

▶ **TEACHER'S RESOURCE GUIDE TOPIC 11 PAGE 78**

1 Desktop Publishing
2 (a) Any three from:
        Printer (ink-jet or laser)
        Scanner
        Digital camera (video or still)
   (b) Printer – to obtain a printout or hardcopy of the document.
        Scanner – to convert any photos or other diagrams to a form that can be stored and manipulated on the computer.
        Digital camera – photographs can be taken and loaded straight into the computer for processing.
3 A template is a document with all the formatting done for you. You only have to add your own text and graphics. Templates save a lot of time and mean that you only have to concentrate on putting in the text and graphics.
4 Any two files from:
   Document files produced using word-processing software.
   Tables, graphs and charts produced using spreadsheet software.
   Image files produced using a digital camera.
   Image files produced using a scanner.
   Clip art from clip art libraries on disk or off the Internet.

Multiple-choice questions

▶ **TEACHER'S RESOURCE GUIDE TOPIC 11 PAGE 79**

1A, 2D, 3A, 4A, 5A, 6C, 7C, 8D, 9D, 10B

▶ Worksheet 1   pp. 132–136

Web and presentation software anagrams

Here are some words or phrases that have been jumbled up. The words are connected with Web and presentation software. Can you work out what they are? There is a clue to help you.

1 Maintain so   *Hint: Moving images are examples of these.*

Answer: _____

2 Nation stirs   *Hint: Movement from one webpage or slide to another.*

Answer: _____

3 Slink   *Hint: You can follow these.*

Answer: _____

4 Mice sponsor   *Hint: Process of reducing file size.*

Answer: _____

5 Lay quit   *Hint: You lose this when images are compressed.*

Answer: _____

6 Lawn dodo   *Hint: It is faster to do this when files are compressed.*

Answer: _____

7 Rat get   *Hint: _____ audience.*

Answer: _____

8 Mask brook   *Hint: Enable users to go back to a webpage/website they like.*

Answer: _____

9 Can trots   *Hint: The difference between the light and dark parts of the screen.*

Answer: _____

10 Sublets it   *Hint: Add these on video for deaf people.*

Answer: _____

▶ Worksheet 2 | pp. 132–136

Creating an evaluation checklist for websites

You have been asked to evaluate a website. Produce a checklist consisting of 20 things you should look for in a good website. Think about the sorts of things you look for in a good website.

1 _____

_____

2 _____

_____

3 _____

_____

4 _____

_____

5 _____

_____

6 _____

_____

7 _____

_____

8 _____

_____

9 _____

_____

10 _____

_____

Worksheet 2 (continued)   pp. 132–136

11 _____

_____

12 _____

_____

13 _____

_____

14 _____

_____

15 _____

_____

16 _____

_____

17 _____

_____

18 _____

_____

19 _____

_____

20 _____

_____

▶ Worksheet 3   pp. 132–136

How much do you know about PowerPoint?

You will be using the presentation software PowerPoint in your GCSE course. You will probably know quite a lot about the software already. See how much basic knowledge you have by answering the following questions on this worksheet.

What do each of the following do?

1   Arial   _____

2   _____

3   A   _____

4   Design   _____

5   _____

6   _____

7   _____

8   _____

9   A   _____

10   _____

▶ Multiple-choice questions

pp. 132–136

1 Pop-up comments on images on a website are mainly used to do which one of the following?

- A Inform the user that they are looking at an image
- B Tell the user the file size
- C Tell the user that the image is being used as a link
- D Open a help screen

2 Animations would *not* include which one of these?

- A A moving banner
- B A moving logo
- C A cartoon
- D A still image from a digital camera

3 A slide transition in a presentation is which one of these?

- A The way one slide replaces another on the screen
- B The way the slides are printed out
- C The way video is used on a slide
- D A way of controlling the volume of sound used

4 A website is aimed at young children. Which one of these statements is correct?

- A Websites should not be used with young children
- B Young children are the target audience
- C Links should not be used
- D Only adults are allowed to use websites

5 Data compression means which one of the following?

- A Decreasing the file size
- B Increasing the file size
- C Copying the file for backup purposes
- D Printing a file

6 Which one of the following is *not* an advantage of data compression?

- A You cannot open the file
- B More files can be stored on the storage media
- C It takes less time to load
- D It can be transferred in less time over the Internet

7 Which one of these is a disadvantage of compressing an image file?

- A It takes less time to send using the Internet
- B The image loses some of its quality
- C The image is turned into black and white
- D You cannot attach it to an email

8 Which one of the following about MP3 files is incorrect?

- A MP3 files are used to store music
- B MP3 files use compression
- C Files in MP3 format take up more space
- D MP3 files are used by portable music players

9 Which one of these is a disadvantage in storing music as MP3 files?

- A You cannot play them using a computer
- B Some of the sound quality is lost owing to the compression
- C You can store lots of them because the file size is small
- D You can copy them to your portable player

10 Which one of these best describes what 'target audience' means?

- A The people who mainly use the website or presentation
- B The people who are unlikely to use the website or presentation
- C Anyone who is able to use a computer
- D Only expert users

ANSWERS

Questions A

▶ **TEXTBOOK PAGE 134**

1 One mark for each point similar to the following to a
   maximum of three marks.
   • They are the people who the website or presentation is
     aimed at (1).
   • They can be different ages (e.g., young children,
     teenagers, young adults, etc.) (1).
   • Then can have a different level of knowledge about the
     subject (e.g., novice, average, expert) (1).
   • Then can have different educational backgrounds (1).

2 One mark for each point to a maximum of three marks.
   • More sophisticated navigation
   • A subtle colour scheme
   • Longer words
   • Careful choice of music or sound
   • Longer sentence length
   • More complex page design

Questions B

▶ **TEXTBOOK PAGE 136**

1 (a) One mark for:
       Storing data in a format that requires less space.
  (b) One mark for:
       More photographs can be stored on the same storage
       media.
       They take less time to transfer over a network.
  (c) One mark for:
       The quality of the photograph is not as high/some of
       the fine detail is lost.

2 (a) One mark for an answer such as:
       • Increase the size of the font used.
       • Use a font type that is easy to read.
       • Use plenty of contrast between the text and the
         background.
       • Allow a user to be able to change the colour scheme.
       • Allow a user to zoom in on certain areas.
       • Use speech synthesis, which reads words out.
  (b) One mark for an answer such as:
       • Display any speech as text.
       • Use visual warnings rather than sounds such as
         beeps.
       • Use subtitles on movies.

Test yourself

▶ **TEXTBOOK PAGE 137**

A animations
B transition
C audience
D standard
E designing
F sizes; types
G displayed

Examination style questions

▶ **TEXTBOOK PAGE 137**

1 (a) One mark for a definition such as:
       The target audience are the people who the website is
       aimed at.

One mark for:
Young children.

  (b) One mark for each item up to a maximum of three
       marks.
       • Large font size – so they can see the letters clearly.
       • Easy to read font type – so they understand how
         letters are formed.
       • Easy navigation – so that they can move around the
         site.
       • No written instructions – as they cannot read.
       • Use of sound to tell them what to do.
       • Use animations to keep them interested.
       • Use of bright colours, which will make the pages
         attractive.

2 (a) One mark for each navigation technique up to a
       maximum of three such as:
       • Forward and back to move to the next or previous
         webpage.
       • Home button to enable users to return to the home
         page.
       • Menus to provide simple ways for the user to make
         selections.
       • Hyperlinks to link to other pages.
       • Bookmarks/favourites to enable users to go back to
         a webpage/website they like.
  (b) One mark for the description and one mark for the
       example.
       Movement of characters, letters, people, etc. For
       example, a cartoon showing letters moving into a
       certain order to make a word.

Worksheet 1: Web and presentation software anagrams

▶ **TEACHER'S RESOURCE GUIDE TOPIC 12 PAGE 82**

1 Animations
2 Transitions
3 Links
4 Compression
5 Quality
6 Download
7 Target
8 Bookmarks
9 Contrast
10 Subtitles

Worksheet 2: Creating an evaluation checklist for websites

▶ **TEACHER'S RESOURCE GUIDE TOPIC 12 PAGE 83**

Here are some of the many possible criteria:
Is the content of the site accurate?
Is the content easy to understand?
Is the content free from spelling and grammatical errors?
Can you tell when the site was last updated?
Is the content kept up-to-date?
Does the site have a search facility?
Is the site easy to navigate?
Do the pages appear overcrowded?
Has colour been used to good effect?
Have appropriate images been included?
Did the site take a long time to load?
Have any annoying animations been included?

Have suitable fonts and font sizes been included?

Do all the links work?

If the links are followed, do they link to relevant and interesting material?

Have long scrolling pages been avoided?

Are there too many pop-up advertisements on the pages?

Is there any useful general information such as the weather on the page?

Is the information on the page in a sensible order?

Does it tell you how many people have viewed the page (i.e., does it include a counter)?

Worksheet 3: How much do you know about PowerPoint?

▶ TEACHER'S RESOURCE GUIDE TOPIC 12 PAGE 85

1 Changes the font type

2 Centres

3 Increases the font size

4 Slide design (pick a template, colour scheme or animation)

5 Create tables or borders

6 Create a text box

7 Slide sorter view

8 Slide show starting from the current slide

9 Font colour

10 Bullet points

Multiple-choice questions

TEACHER'S RESOURCE GUIDE TOPIC 12 PAGE 86

1C, 2D, 3A, 4B, 5A, 6A, 7B, 8C, 9B, 10A

▶ Worksheet 1   p. 144

Features of websites

There are common features to most websites. In this activity you will be tested on the purposes of these common features.

For each of the following features, you need to explain why they have been included.

1   SITE MAP

2   HELP

3   09:29:55

4
VISITORS

5   Useful Links

6   Welcome

7   Message board

8   [   ] search

9   Home

10   Copyright

▶ Worksheet 2

p. 145

Web icons

Web icons are small pictures used in websites to perform an action or act as a link. Good web icons are icons where it is fairly obvious what they do.

See if you can write down what the purpose of each of the following web icons is?

1

Answer: _____

2

Answer: _____

▶ Worksheet 2 (continued)   p. 145

3

Answer: _____

4

Answer: _____

5

Answer: _____

6

Answer: _____

7

Answer: _____

8

Answer: _____

▶ Worksheet 2 (continued)   p. 145

9

Answer: _____

10

Answer: _____

▶ Worksheet 3   pp. 144–147

Worksheet 3: Web software anagrams

Here are some words or phrases that have been jumbled up. The words are connected with Web software. Can you work out what they are? There is a clue to help you.

1 Metal pet   *Hint: Use this so you don't have to worry about design.*

Answer: _____

2 Mega hope   *Hint: Usually the first page of a website.*

Answer: _____

3 Barn en   *Hint: A rectangular area used for advertising.*

Answer: _____

4 Yelp shrink   *Hint: Another name for links.*

Answer: _____

5 Mask brook   *Hint: Used to mark a good website you might want to return to.*

Answer: _____

6 Cattleman thief   *Hint: The file you attach to an email is called this.*

Answer: _____

7 Shot top   *Hint: Part of a website that acts as a link.*

Answer: _____

8 Bacon cry op   *Hint: An exact copy.*

Answer: _____

9 Dreads books   *Hint: Where you keep your addresses.*

Answer: _____

10 Amps   *Hint: Unwanted email.*

Answer: _____

▶ Multiple-choice questions

pp. 144–147

1 URL stands for which one of the following?

A Uniform regional locator
B Uniform resource locator
C Unified resource locator
D United reference loss

2 Which one of the following is *not* an interactive feature of a website?

A Online form
B Game
C Quiz
D Text

3 In website design software, a skeleton structure of the design for all the pages of a website where you simply add your own content is called which one of the following?

A A frame
B A template
C A hyperlink
D A home page

4 When you type a URL into a web browser you are directed to the first page of a website. What is this first page called?

A The home page
B The flat page
C The regular page
D The single page

5 On a website which one of these is a leader board?

A An advert on a website
B A heading on a webpage
C The first page you come to on a website
D A map of what is on the site

6 HTML stands for which one of the following?

A Hypertext Markup Language
B Hypertext Markup Locator
C Hypertext Making Language
D Nothing

7 The connection between one webpage and another is called which one of these?

A Hypertext
B Link
C Home page
D Browser

8 RGB stands for which one of the following?

A Really Good Backup
B Red Green Black
C Red Green Blue
D Red Green Banner

9 Web icons are which one of these?

A Small pictures on websites to indicate a link or action
B Any image on a website
C Photographs that are compressed
D Any famous person who has their own website

10 www.folens.com is an example of which one of these?

A URL
B HTML
C GIGO
D BMP

ANSWERS

Questions A

▶ **TEXTBOOK PAGE 143**

1 (a) One mark each to a maximum of two marks.
   - They can type in the URL of a website where the information can be found and then use a key search on the website
   - They can use a search engine and type in a few key words or a phrase about the information they are looking for

   (b) One mark each for two of the following:
   - Online forms
   - Questionnaires
   - Emails
   - Message boards/comments
   - Games
   - Quizzes
   - Email

2 (a) One mark for Hypertext Markup Language
   (b) One mark for:
      Use web development software

Questions B

▶ **TEXTBOOK PAGE 147**

1 One mark for each point to a maximum of three marks.
   - A template is a pre-designed series of webpages forming a website (1)
   - It contains all the design aspects (font types, font sizes, backgrounds, navigation, etc.)
   - It contains all the links between the pages
   - All you have to do is add your own content

2 (a) One mark for an explanation such as:
      An image or piece of text used as a link
   (b) One mark for:
      A rectangular area on the webpage that acts as an advert, so when a user clicks on the area, they are taken to the advertiser's site

Test yourself

▶ **TEXTBOOK PAGE 148**

A URL, address
B Hyperlinks
C anchor
D website
E web browser
F web servers

Examination style questions

▶ **TEXTBOOK PAGE 148**

1 One mark for each name and one mark for a brief description of purpose × 2.
   - Web browser (1) enables a user to search for information on the Internet and to access webpages (1).
   - Web development software (1) used to create websites by adding navigation, links, banners, etc. (1).

2 (a) One mark for: It is an image that also acts as a link. When you click on it you follow the link.
   (b) One mark for: It is used in long webpages where the user need not read all the text to get to the bit they want.

They simply click on a menu that takes them to the point on the same webpage where the information is.
   (c) One mark for: The button changes its appearance when the cursor is moved over it and it acts as a link.

Worksheet 1: Features of websites

▶ **TEACHER'S RESOURCE GUIDE TOPIC 13 PAGE 89**

1 A user can see exactly what is on the site quickly.
2 Provides additional assistance should the user get into difficulty in using the website.
3 Gives the exact local time so that users can see the exact time in the website owner's country. This is particularly useful if you wanted to contact them by telephone.
4 Counter showing the number of people who have visited the site. This is useful for the website owner to see how popular their site is and also for the visitors to see how important the site is.
5 Provides a quick way for the user to go to a series of suggested websites that may be useful to them.
6 Provides a brief introduction to the website and outlines its purpose and aims.
7 Provides a way for users to leave messages so that other users of the site can comment on them.
8 Provides a quick way of searching the website using a series of key words.
9 Provides a quick way for the user to go back to the home page of the site.
10 Provides copyright information. This may or may not give users permission to use some of the content on the site on their own site.

Worksheet 2: Web icons

▶ **TEACHER'S RESOURCE GUIDE TOPIC 13 PAGE 90**

1 Home
2 Shopping/buy item
3 Forward
4 Print
5 Help
6 Email
7 Search
8 Refresh
9 Add to favourites
10 Security

Worksheet 3: Web software anagrams

▶ **TEACHER'S RESOURCE GUIDE TOPIC 13 PAGE 94**

1 Template
2 Home page
3 Banner
4 Hyperlinks
5 Bookmarks
6 File attachment
7 Hotspot
8 Carbon copy
9 Address book
10 Spam

Multiple-choice questions

▶ **TEACHER'S RESOURCE GUIDE TOPIC 13 PAGE 95**

1B, 2D, 3B, 4A, 5A, 6A, 7B, 8C, 9A, 10A

Mind maps on presentation software

Read pages 151–154 of the textbook and then complete the following mind maps.

Advantages of presentation software

Disadvantages of presentation software

▶ Activity 1 | pp. 152–154

Adding a sound file to a PowerPoint presentation

1 Load PowerPoint.

2 Create a New Blank Presentation or Open an existing presentation.

3 Click on the slide on which you want to record the sound.

4 You can now either:

  • Insert a sound clip from a file. You will need a previous saved sound clip for this. Click on **Insert** then **Movies and Sounds** and finally **Sound from File**. You will then be presented with a screen to find and then insert the sound file.

    OR

  • Insert a sound from the Clip Organiser. Click on **Insert** then **Movies and Sounds** and finally **Sound from Clip Organiser**. You are then presented with a list of the available sound clips from which to choose.

5 The following message appears:

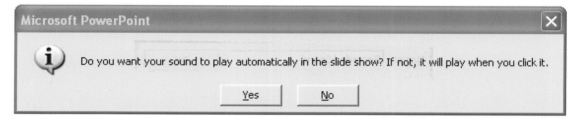

  If you want the sound to play automatically, click on Yes and if not, click on No.

6 To preview the sound, double click on the loudspeaker icon.

  Important *note*
  When you add sound to your presentation, the sound file is not stored with the presentation. Instead it is linked to it. It is important to know this because if you copy the presentation, you will need to make sure that the sound clips are copied as well.

▶ Activity 2 | pp. 152–154

Recording narration on a slide

In this activity you will record a narration for a slide show. A narration allows you to record you talking about each slide. This is very useful if your slide show is to be viewed by a user without you being present.

Before you try to record any sound, check that you have a microphone connected. Most laptop computers have a microphone built in but with desktop computers, you will need to connect one unless someone else has already done this.

Tip

Before starting the narration for each slide, it is a good idea to write down a script. You can then refine this script and read from it when recording the narration.

1   Load PowerPoint.

2   Create a New Blank Presentation or Open an existing presentation.

3   Click on the slide on which you want to record the narration.

4   Click on **Insert** then on **Movies and Sounds** and finally on **Record Sound**.

5   The following window appears:

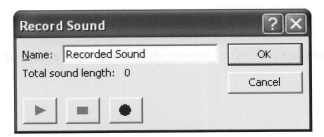

6   You can change the Name of the recorded sound to give it a more meaningful name. In this case the name of the sound has been changed to Introduction.

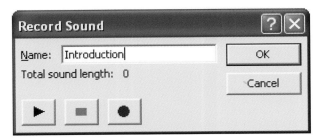

7   Notice the Action Buttons on the slide. Here is what they mean:

 Play

Stop

Record

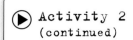 **Activity 2** pp. 152–154
(continued)

Click on Record and then say the following:

'When recording voice narration you need to be in a quiet room so that no background noise will distract the user of the presentation. Speak clearly and talk slowly. Also, make sure there is no-one around, otherwise they may think you are talking to yourself!'

As soon as you have stopped talking, click on the **Stop** button and then click on **OK**.

You will then see the loudspeaker icon ◀ on the screen. If this icon is in the way of some content, then it may be dragged to a more convenient position. You can also alter the size of the icon using the handles.

8 To hear the sound you need to run the presentation and then click on the loudspeaker icon when it appears.

9 To add narration to other slides, you simply repeat these steps.

Important *note*
Narration is embedded into the PowerPoint file. This means that the sound files are saved as part of the presentation.

▶ Activity 3 | pp. 152–154

Inserting an audio track from a CD onto a slide

It is easy to insert an audio track from a CD onto a slide. Beware though – consider your audience – your choice of music may not be theirs!

1   Load PowerPoint.

2   Insert the CD from which you want the track into the CD-player.

3   Create a New Blank Presentation or Open an existing presentation.

4   Click on the slide on which you want to record the track from the CD.

5   Click on **Insert** then on **Movies and Sounds** and finally on **Play CD Audio Track**.

The following window appears:

You can now select the start track and end track. Usually these will be the same, but it is possible to play several tracks on the same slide.
You will need to experiment with the timings, so that you get the section of the music you want. Note that you need not start at the beginning of the track.

6   When you have made your selections, click on **OK**.

The following window appears:

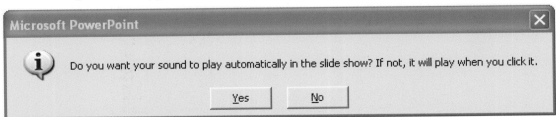

If you click Yes, the music will play automatically and if you click No, the user will have to click on the CD icon to hear it.

7   You can now run the presentation to test it.

▶ **Activity 4** pp. 152–154

Producing a group presentation on UFOs

For this activity you will research and then do a group presentation on UFOs (unidentified flying objects). The research will be done using the Internet where you will search for text, pictures, sounds, video, etc., that you can use to build your presentation. The purpose of this activity is to show off your skills in the material you have covered in the following topics:

Topic 12 Web and presentation software

Topic 14 Presentation software.

Your audience for the presentation will be Year 11 students, although your teacher will be present to assess you.

Some people believe in UFOs and some don't. You will work in a group to produce a presentation about UFOs. The presentation must last between 5 and 10 minutes.

You could:
- Take the view that you believe that UFOs exist.
- Take the view that you do not believe that UFOs exist.
- Take an open view and let the audience make up their own minds.

Before you start, you will need to discuss with your group members:
- Which one of the above approaches you will use.
- How to break down the overall task into smaller tasks.
- How to choose who should do each of the smaller tasks.
- If you are each producing slides, how you can ensure consistency from one slide to another.

Important *notes*

Use the skills of your group so you need to have a discussion as to what each member of your group is best at.

▶ **Activity 4** (continued) | pp. 152–154

Researching your material

Use the Internet and a suitable search engine to find websites on UFOs.

When searching the Internet you would probably start by typing in UFO as your key word condition. Think about as many aspects of the subject (i.e. UFOs) as you can. You can put them in a diagram like this:

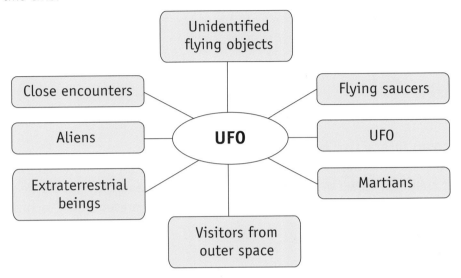

Try to think of all the aspects of a subject such as UFOs by drawing a diagram like this.

Use the above diagram (or one you have produced yourselves) to help with your searches.

As well as the text, you will also need to make sure that you can find some of the following to include in your presentation:

- images
- sounds/music
- video – you may be able to find some actual video of UFO sightings.

You will also need to consider the following to make your presentation exciting to your target audience:

- slide transitions
- animations.

Delivering the presentation

Your group will present the information on UFOs using the slides to your teacher and the rest of the group. Here are some tips:

- Practise your presentation thoroughly.
- Time your presentation to make sure that it lasts between 5 and 7 minutes.
- Try not to read from notes.
- Maintain eye contact with your audience.
- As you are working in a group, choose the most confident person/persons to do the talking.

You could also consider adding narration to your slides. This means the presentation could be self-running so that all you have to do is to introduce the presentation and answer any questions your audience has at the end.

▶ Extension activity | pp. 152–154

Halloween presentation

Task 1: Collecting sounds for a Halloween self-running presentation

For this activity you have to collect 20 sounds that could be used in a Halloween multimedia product for young children. Store the sounds in a folder called Halloween.

You can use any source of sound files, but you may find good ones on the www.findsounds.com website. You will need to think about the wording of the search conditions to find appropriate sound files. Here are some to start you off:

1   Creaky door

2   An owl hooting

3   A witch's cackle

Task 2: Creating an interactive Halloween presentation

You now have to create an interactive Halloween presentation for young children.

The idea is that they will view the presentation on their own and they should be able to choose what they do next. Use all the multimedia effects and presentation techniques that are appropriate.

▶ Multiple-choice questions | pp. 152–154

1 A feature of a presentation that allows a user to jump to another slide by clicking on an area on the slide is called which one of these?

A Cold spot
B Hotspot
C Area
D Blog

2 Most presentations make use of multimedia. Which one best describes the meaning of the word multimedia?

A Making use of many media such as text, still images, sound, video, etc.
B Making use of one type of media
C A type of DTP package
D A hardware device

3 Navigate means which one of these?

A To copy a slide
B The way a slide appears on the screen
C To move from one slide to another
D To print a slide

4 Which one of the following is *not* an output device used with a presentation package?

A Screen
B Printer
C Speakers
D Robot arm

5 A line of text or words with a symbol placed in front so it stands out is called which one of these?

A Shot point
B Shell point
C Bullet point
D Rocket point

6 A slide transition is which one of these?

A The way one slide is copied
B The way notes are printed out
C The way one slide disappears and another slide appears on the screen
D The way one slide is linked to another using hyperlinks

7 Which one of the following *cannot* be added to a slide in a presentation?

A Music
B Video
C Still images
D Smell

8 Which one of the following is a brand name for presentation software?

A PowerRangers
B Access
C Excel
D PowerPoint

9 Slide timing means which one of these?

A The time a slide takes to create
B The time a slide is on the screen before it is automatically replaced by another
C The time a slide takes to print
D The time for the slide to arrive through the post

10 The hardware needed when recording a slide narration is which one of these?

A Speakers
B Microphone
C Printer
D Digital camera

ANSWERS

Questions A

▶ TEXTBOOK PAGE 154

1 (a) One mark for:
   A hyperlink is an icon/graphic/word on a document (slide or webpage) that, when clicked with the mouse, opens another slide or webpage.
   (b) One mark for:
   An area which when clicked on acts as a link.
   It can be an image, part of an image, a button or text.
2 (a) One mark for:
   The way one slide is replaced by another.
   (b) One mark for:
   The way content moves in order to appear on the slide.

Test yourself

▶ TEXTBOOK PAGE 155

A design template
B Animation
C bullet
D transition
E navigation
F hyperlink
G hotspots

Examination style questions

▶ TEXTBOOK PAGE 155

1 (a) One mark for each of two points similar to the following:
   Templates are partly prepared documents/slides that contain placeholder text and graphics (1), which you can replace with your own to save you from starting from scratch (1)
   (b) One mark for one of the following:
   • It is much faster
   • You do not have to worry about the design and only need to concentrate on the content
   (c) One mark for one of the following:
   • The audience may have seen the design many times
   • There may not be a suitable design template
2 (a) One mark for an answer such as:
   You need to leave enough time for the viewer to read and understand what is on each slide
   (b) One mark for an answer such as:
   • This is speech that explains each slide, that has been prepared and saved on the computer, which is played back when each slide is shown (1)
   • The preparer of the presentation does not have to be present (1)

Multiple-choice questions

▶ TEACHER'S RESOURCE GUIDE TOPIC 14 PAGE 105

1B, 2A, 3C, 4D, 5C, 6C, 7D, 8D, 9B, 10B

▶ Worksheet 1   pp. 160–166

Multimedia anagrams

Here are some words or phrases that have been jumbled up. The words are connected with Multimedia. Can you work out what they are? There is a clue to help you.

1   Outlines or   *Hint: A measure of how clear an image appears.*

    Answer: _____

2   Dial tie mum   *Hint: Means many media.*

    Answer: _____

3   Creativity tin   *Hint: The user can decide what they do next.*

    Answer: _____

4   More my   *Hint: Having a large amount of this is important for multimedia.*

    Answer: _____

5   Breaking cost   *Hint: Storage that is not main memory is called this.*

    Answer: _____

6   Maybe get   *Hint: 1024 kilobytes.*

    Answer: _____

7   Manacle press   *Hint: Large flat panel screen.*

    Answer: _____

8   Birthplace tags   *Hint: You can draw freehand on a tablet.*

    Answer: _____

9   Cipher mono   *Hint: Input device used for sound.*

    Answer: _____

10   Became war   *Hint: Sometimes situated at the top of a computer screen.*

    Answer: _____

▶ **Activity**

pp. 165–166

Creating a multimedia Christmas or birthday card

Create a multimedia Christmas or birthday card using presentation software (e.g. PowerPoint).

Ensure that your card uses multimedia features such as:

- text
- sound
- images
- animation – if you can work out how to do this.

▶ Multiple-choice questions pp. 160–166

1 Multimedia is used in education. The main reason for this is which one of these?

A It is the 'in' thing
B It uses many different ways of presenting material, which suits learners
C There are not enough teachers
D It is expensive

2 Which one of these devices could be used to input a file of someone talking about a product into a webpage?

A Graphics tablet
B Touch screen
C Microphone
D Speaker

3 Which one of the following is *not* a multimedia feature?

A Sound
B Animation
C Interactivity
D Traditional paper books

4 Which one of the following is *not* an advantage of multimedia software?

A It is usually mass produced so it is cheap
B It uses many different types of media
C It can be used in many different ways
D You cannot use it on a laptop computer

5 Which of the following is a disadvantage of multimedia software?

A It can be distracting to others who are nearby and want some peace
B You can learn a whole range of subjects using multimedia software
C It appeals to all ages
D It makes boring subjects come alive

6 Which of the following statements is false?

A MIDI is an interface
B Multimedia software uses a lot of memory
C Multimedia software needs a lot of storage
D Multimedia cannot be used in business

7 Which of the following statements is true?

A A digital video camera can be used to input video into a package
B A mouse is an output device
C Webcams are output devices
D Digital photographs cannot be re-sized

8 Which one of these statements is false?

A ROM and RAM are types of memory
B Programs are stored in memory when they are being used
C Multimedia needs lots of memory
D It is impossible to have more than one program open at the same time

9 A website has been produced that includes multimedia features. Which one of the following is *not* a multimedia feature?

A Sound
B Interactivity
C Video
D Microphone

10 A multimedia quiz has been produced to check students' understanding of a topic. Which one of the following is it *not* likely to include?

A Interactivity
B Video
C Sound
D Robots

ANSWERS

Activity: Spotting multimedia components in websites

▶ **TEXTBOOK PAGE 160**

1 Images – graphics such as the Ferrari logo, photographs such as pictures of cars.
Animation – moving text, graphics showing loading information, moving cars, roof opening/closing, etc.
Text – explanations of the cars, instructions on how to use the site, etc.
Interactive buttons – to make selections, open and shut roofs on cars, etc.

2 Text – explanations of the Premier League, instructions for use of website, etc.
Graphics – pictures of footballers, managers, club emblems, etc.
Animations – moving text, interactive games (when you register).
Sound – on the interactive games (these are free but you need to register).
Interactive buttons – to make selections.

3 Text – stories, advertisements, etc.
Graphics – photographs, pictures of products.
Video – there is a webcam where you can see what is going on in the office.
Interactive buttons – to make selections.

Questions A

▶ **TEXTBOOK PAGE 161**

1 Any three (one mark each) from: images/graphics, audio/sound, video, movies/animation, interactive buttons/interactivity.

2 Any three sensible components (one mark each) such as: today's date, date last updated, counter showing number of visitors, email, site map, help, copyright information, etc.

3 One mark each for three items such as:
- Sounds/music that you cannot turn off when you are browsing a website.
- Flash graphics that take ages to load, especially if you do not have broadband.
- Websites with lots of flashy graphics that do not tell you the information you are looking for.
- Websites that use text that is difficult to read, because the wrong font has been used.
- Websites with the wrong use of combinations of background and font colours.
- Websites that contain links that do not work.
- Websites that cause your computer to crash.
- Websites containing material that is incorrect.
- Websites that contain mistakes in grammar or spelling.

Questions B

▶ **TEXTBOOK PAGE 164**

1 (a) One mark for each tick in the correct place (i.e. a maximum of five marks).

	Tick 5 boxes only
Graphics tablet	√
Colour laser printer	
Mouse	√
Microphone	√
Speakers	
LCD screen	
Pen drive	
Digital still camera	√
Magnetic hard disk drive	
CD-ROM drive	
Webcam	√

(b) One mark for each output device to a maximum of two marks.
- Colour laser printer
- LCD screen
- Speakers

(c) One mark for one of the following:
- Magnetic hard disk drive
- CD-ROM drive
- Pen drive

2 (a) One mark for: Musical Instrument Digital <u>Interface</u>
(b) One mark for a point such as one of the following:
- MIDI is an interface, which means a way of connecting and getting two devices to communicate with each other
- A way of saving music from a music instrument on a computer

Questions C

▶ **TEXTBOOK PAGE 166**

1 (a) One mark for a reference to entering a word or a few words that describe what the user is looking for.
(b) One mark for each interactive component to a maximum of two marks.
- Keyword searches
- Quizzes
- Questionnaires
- Polls
- Games
- Links

2 (a) One mark for an answer similar to the following: Pre-stored images that you can take and use in your own material.
(b) One mark each for two of the following:
- Use the clip art provided with the software package
- Use a CD-ROM or DVD containing a huge amount of clip art
- Use the Internet to access online clip art libraries

Topic 15 Multimedia

Test yourself

▶ TEXTBOOK PAGE 167

A media
B interactivity
C Animations
D websites
E broadband
F memory, upgraded
G Video

Examination style questions

▶ TEXTBOOK PAGE 167

1 (a) One mark each for any three features from:
  • Text
  • Still images/photographs
  • Animation/cartoons
  • Video
  • Audio
  • Interactive components (or an interactive component, e.g. links)
  (b) One mark for one answer similar to the following (NB one word answers are not enough here).
  • Can show a video of their product working
  • Can use voice to explain the product
  • Can produce an eye-catching animation to keep users interested in the advert
  • Can use text so that users can read about the benefits of the product
  (c) One mark for one disadvantage such as:
  • It takes time to create multimedia pages
  • They may not have the skills needed to create the pages
  • The user may not have the hardware needed to use the multimedia put on the pages

2 (a) Two marks for a definition similar to the following, that makes two points.
  Multimedia means many media (1) such as text, audio, still images, animation, video and interactivity (1)
  (b) One mark each for two input devices such as:
  • Graphics tablet
  • Touch screen
  • Light pen
  • Scanner
  • Microphone
  • Music player (e.g., MP3 player, i-Pod, etc.)

3 There are many possible answers here. The one being described here is a travel company website. One mark for each distinctly different point to a maximum of six such as:
  • Text to explain the site and give instructions how to use it
  • Interactivity – such as a search facility that lets users search for holidays according to date, area, type of holiday, etc.
  • Interactivity such as links to maps such as Google Earth that show the vicinity of the hotel, etc.
  • Online questionnaires – that allow holidaymakers to fill in their answers to questions
  • Text – reviews and scores for accommodation, resort, food, etc.

  • Audio – can be used for people with poor eyesight so that any text can be read out to them
  • Video – a video of the hotel and its facilities
  • Animation – an animated logo of the holiday company is shown on the screen
  • Graphics – photographs of places of interest are shown
  • Audio – people discussing their holiday
  • Talk to a representative – this is where a user can conduct a conversation with a booking representative using a service similar to instant messaging
  • Site map – to let a user quickly know what is on the website

4 One mark for each point to a maximum of four marks similar to the following:
  • Many images of the same thing can be taken (1) and the best one chosen (1)
  • If you copy and paste images taken by someone else, you could be infringing copyright (1), but if you take them yourself, you do not have this problem (1)
  • Images can be edited to improve their appearance (1) For example, a person with spots on their face can have the spots removed for a final image (1)
  • Images can be edited (1) such as re-sizing so they fit a space in the design of a webpage (1)

5 One mark for each point to a maximum of four marks along similar lines to the following:
  • Can show a car, and the user can select colours for body, upholstery, etc. (1)
  • Users can select different views of the car (1)
  • Users can zoom in on different parts of the car they are interested in (1)
  • Users can see animations of how certain controls of the car work (1)
  • User can experience a driver's view of the car in a video (1)
  • Users can customize their car by adding optional extras (1)
  • Users can hear audio of owners discussing how they found their new car (1)
  • Can have links to reviews of the cars in online car magazines (1)

Worksheet 1: Multimedia anagrams

▶ TEACHER'S RESOURCE GUIDE TOPIC 15 PAGE 107

1 Resolution
2 Multimedia
3 Interactivity
4 Memory
5 Backing store
6 Megabyte
7 Plasma screen
8 Graphics tablet
9 Microphone
10 Web camera

Multiple-choice questions

▶ TEACHER'S RESOURCE GUIDE TOPIC 15 PAGE 109

1B, 2C, 3D, 4D, 5A, 6D, 7A, 8D, 9D, 10D

▶ Activity   pp. 174–175

What do these buttons do in a graphics package?

Here are the meanings of the buttons. You have to write the meaning of each button next to it.

- Draw a rectangle
- Draw a curve
- Insert text
- Airbrush
- Fill with colour (flood fill)
- Draw a line
- Magnify
- Pencil
- Paintbrush

1 _____

2 _____

3 _____

4 _____

5 _____

6 _____

7 _____

8 _____

9 _____

Worksheet pp. 172–178

Digital imaging anagrams

Here are some words or phrases that have been jumbled up. The words are connected with Digital imaging. Can you work out what they are? There is a clue to help you.

1 Covert *Hint: One of the two main types of image.*

Answer: _____

2 Bait pm *Hint: The other type of image.*

Answer: _____

3 Rat toe *Hint: A type of transformation.*

Answer: _____

4 Cling as *Hint: Sizing to a certain pre-determined size.*

Answer: _____

5 Angry lie *Hint: Useful for animation.*

Answer: _____

6 Late pet *Hint: Collection of colours to choose from.*

Answer: _____

7 Grind tea *Hint: Effect where the colour starts to fade.*

Answer: _____

8 Edit gin *Hint: Name for the process of altering an image in some way.*

Answer: _____

9 Septic moo *Hint: Repeating pattern.*

Answer: _____

10 Harp got hop? *Hint: JPEG file format is good for this*

Answer: _____

▶ Multiple-choice questions pp. 172–178

1 Which one of the following best describes a pixel?

A It is a type of graphic
B It is a piece of software
C It is the smallest dot of light that can appear on a computer screen
D It is a type of printer

2 Which one of the following statements about bitmaps is incorrect?

A Bitmap graphics take up more storage than vector graphics
B They can become blurred when enlarged
C They are made up of pixels
D Photographic images are not bitmaps

3 Which one of the following statements is false?

A Bitmap images are made up of pixels
B Vector images can be resized without loss of quality
C It is impossible to resize a bitmap image
D Photographic images are examples of bitmaps

4 Which of the following is a graphic that is expressed mathematically as an equation or set of equations?

A Bitmap graphic
B Vector graphic
C Tiptop graphic
D Backdrop graphic

5 The number of pixels per inch is called which one of these?

A Screen resolution
B Screen width
C Screen size
D Bitmap

6 A graphic or image stored as a map showing the position and colour of individual dots of light on the screen is called which one of these?

A A vector graphic
B A bitmap graphic
C A mapped graphic
D A road mapped graphic

7 When you publish an image on a website it is called which one of these?

A Copying
B Backing up
C Uploading
D Downloading

8 When an image on a webpage in passed over the Internet to the user's computer it is called which one of these?

A Copying
B Backing up
C Uploading
D Downloading

9 When an image is to be published on a website it should be optimized.

Which of these is a reason why the image needs to be optimized?

A It should be turned into a file that uses compression, which will make it faster to load

B So that it can be saved easily

C So that hackers cannot access the file

D To make sure that the file is encrypted

10 Which one of the following about a vector image is false?

A They can be enlarged without loss in quality

B The image itself is not stored

C Sets of equations are used to draw the graphic

D Photographic images are always vector graphics

ANSWERS

Questions A

▶ **TEXTBOOK PAGE 173**

1 (a) One mark for one of the following:
- Scanner
- Mouse
- Light pen
- Graphics tablet

(b) One mark for: Bitmap graphic

(c) One mark for each point to a maximum of two marks.
- Graphic made up of an arrangement of pixels
- Whose position is stored as a map of the pixels
- Also stored is further information about the colours of each pixel

(d) One mark for each point to a maximum of two marks.
- A graphic which is formed by geometric objects
- The equations to draw these objects are stored
- The image itself is not stored

(e) One mark for each point to a maximum of two marks.
- Can be resized without loss in image quality
- Does not take as long to upload or download using the Internet as the file size is smaller
- Smaller file sizes means it is possible to store more files on the same media
- Vectors allow you to zoom in and out
- It is possible to transform the image (e.g., rotate, reflect, etc.)

Questions B

▶ **TEXTBOOK PAGE 176**

1 (a) One mark for each point to a maximum of two marks such as:
- Increased or decreased in size
- So that the image is increased or decreased in size in both directions by the same amount
- So that the image is not distorted
- Increased or decreased in size by a percentage 150%, 50%, etc.

(b) One mark for each point to a maximum of three marks such as:
- Rotated
- Reflected
- Cropped
- Sized

2 (a) One mark for bitmap.
(b) One mark for vector.
(c) One mark for vector.
(d) One mark for vector.
(e) One mark for bitmap.

Questions C

▶ **TEXTBOOK PAGE 178**

1 (a) One mark for each point to a maximum of two marks.
- Graphic made up of an arrangement of pixels
- Whose position is stored as a map of the pixels
- Also stored is further information about the colours of each pixel

(b) One mark for each point to a maximum of two marks.
- High resolution image appears sharper
- High resolution contains more pixels

- The pixels are small so you cannot see them
- Diagonal lines do not appear jagged

2 One mark for a reason such as:
- To reduce the file size
- So that the file can be uploaded/downloaded using the Internet in less time
- So that more files can be stored on the storage media

3 One mark each for two of the following:
- bmp
- jpeg
- gif
- tiff
- eps
- png
- psd

Test yourself

▶ **TEXTBOOK PAGE 179**

A pixel
B bitmap
C upload, download
D vector
E quality
F pixels
G resolution
H bitmap
I JPEG

Examination style questions

▶ **TEXTBOOK PAGE 179**

1 One mark for each of two ways such as:
- Resized
- Cropped
- Contrast
- Brightness
- Red eye removed
- Airbrushed/individual pixels altered
- Colour adjustment
- Transformed
- Rotated
- Reflected
- Stretched
- Etc.

2 (a) One mark for: Transparent
(b) One mark for the tool and one mark for a description × 2.
- Crop – cut away an unwanted section of an image
- Reflection – create one image and then create another facing the other way
- Resize – make an image fit in a space on a webpage

3 One mark for each point up to a maximum of four marks.
Vector graphic
- Image not stored (1)
- Only the instructions/equations to create the image (1)
- Each part of the image can be edited individually (1)
- Small file size (1)
- Resulting fast upload/download (1)

Bitmap graphic
- Details of pixels are stored (i.e., position and colour) (1)

- Resulting file size is large (1)
- Harder to edit image (1)
- Resizing degrades image (1)
- Uploading/downloading takes longer (1)
- Need to use a file format that compresses the bitmap (1)

Activity: What do these buttons do in a graphics package?

▶ TEACHER'S RESOURCE GUIDE TOPIC 16 PAGE 112

1 Airbrush
2 Fill with colour (flood fill)
3 Insert text
4 Magnify
5 Draw a line
6 Pencil
7 Paintbrush
8 Draw a curve
9 Draw a rectangle

Worksheet: Digital imaging anagrams

▶ TEACHER'S RESOURCE GUIDE TOPIC 16 PAGE 113

1 Vector
2 Bitmap
3 Rotate
4 Scaling
5 Layering
6 Palette
7 Gradient
8 Editing
9 Composite
10 Photograph

Multiple-choice questions

▶ TEACHER'S RESOURCE GUIDE TOPIC 16 PAGE 114

1C, 2D, 3C, 4B, 5A, 6B, 7C, 8D, 9A, 10D

▶ Worksheet

Animation anagrams

Here are some words or phrases that have been jumbled up. The words are connected with Animation. Can you work out what they are? There is a clue to help you.

1 Presence sit   *Hint: _____ of vision.*

Answer: _____

2 Bop folk I   *Hint: Animation where you flip a book.*

Answer: _____

3 Motion post   *Hint: You move the object take a picture, move it again take a picture and so on.*

Answer: _____

4 Freaky me   *Hint: Type of animation where you have a start and end frame.*

Answer: _____

5 Teen wing   *Hint: Putting in the in-between frames.*

Answer: _____

6 Vial rut   *Hint: _____ learning environment.*

Answer: _____

7 Go lo   *Hint: Graphic used to identify an organization.*

Answer: _____

8 Ban be wren   *Hint: A form of advertising on websites.*

Answer: _____

9 Retold free   *Hint: A graphic representation of a file structure.*

Answer: _____

10 Yard robots   *Hint: Used to explain how an animation, multimedia presentation or website will work.*

Answer: _____

► **Activity 1** | pp. 186–189

Animating pictures and text in PowerPoint presentation software

One simple way of moving text or a whole picture is to use the animation techniques in PowerPoint. Follow these steps:

1 Load the PowerPoint software.

2 Select a layout that gives you a completely blank slide.

3 Add a picture to the slide (this can be clip art or any image).

4 Click on the picture and using the handles re-size the image so that it is about 3 cm square. Your screen will now look similar to this (with your own image inserted).

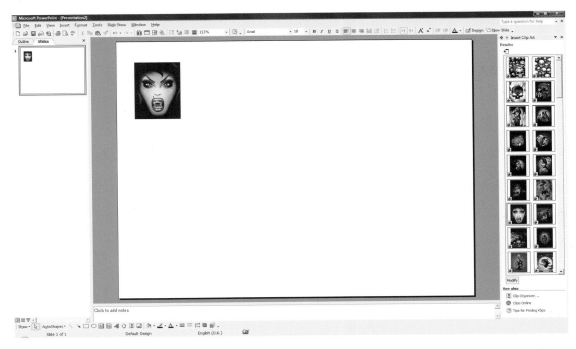

5 Open the Slide Show menu and click on Custom Animation and the following panel can be seen at the right of the screen.

► **Activity 1**
(continued)

pp. 186–189

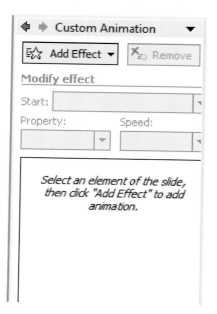

6   Click on Add Effects.
    From the menu that appears select Entrance and from the next menu select Fly In.

7   Notice the following appears on the right of the screen.

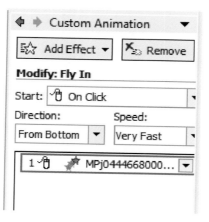

    Notice you can change what starts the animation (in this case the user clicking) and also
    the direction in which the image travels and also the speed.

8   You can now play your animation in the way a user would see it by clicking on the play
    button at the bottom right of the screen.

9   Save your animation using a suitable filename.

▶ Activity 2 | pp. 186–189

Experimenting with animation effects in PowerPoint

There are lots of effects you can do using animation using PowerPoint presentation software.

For this activity you are required to experiment with the techniques.

Here are some of the things you can try:
- Find out how to make the image come on to the page from different directions (e.g., from bottom, from left, from top right, etc.).
- Find out how to alter the speed of the animation.
- Find out how to get the picture to follow a path that you draw on the slide. Note that this is called a motion path.
- Find out how to add an emphasis (e.g., spin where the image comes onto the page and then makes one revolution or where it grows and then shrinks).
- Find out how to make the image go off the page (i.e. exit).

▶ Activity 3 | pp. 186–189

Producing a storyboard for an animation

You are planning but not producing an animation for young children.

The animation is going to accompany the text of a nursery rhyme.

You have to find a simple nursery rhyme (use the Internet to find one).

Produce a storyboard for the animation.

In your storyboard you will need to say what text and images should appear on each frame and also what the animation shows.

▶ Multiple-choice questions

pp. 184–191

1 Books containing a slightly different drawing on each page, which appears to move when the pages are flipped quickly, are called which one of these?

A Flick books
B Flip books
C Rotoscopes
D 3D images

2 The human eye sees an object for a small amount of time after the object has disappeared. This is called which one of these?

A Persistence of vision
B Tunnel vision
C Stereo vision
D Mono vision

3 What is the reason that frames, when played at a certain rate, show smooth motion?

A Tweening
B Key frame animation
C VLE
D Persistence of vision

4 Which one of the following about 3D animation is correct?

A It is easy to produce using a flip book
B Special 3D animation software is needed to produce it
C It is not as complicated to produce as 2D animation
D It is impossible to produce 3D animation

5 Which one of the following statements is false?

A Stop motion animation uses a model
B The model is moved slightly and photographed for each frame
C The frames are joined together to form the animation
D The motion appears very jerky

6 Another name for tweening is which one of these?

A Outbetweening
B Inbetweening
C Rotoscoping
D Rollerblading

7 What does GIF stand for?

A Graphics interchange format
B Graphics interface format
C Graphics idiot free
D Garbage in garbage out

8 Adobe Flash is a software package used for which one of these?

A Word processing
B Animation
C Spreadsheet
D Database creation

9 Which one of the following is *not* a file format used for animation?

A gif
B png
C cgm
D doc

10 Creating a start and end frame and then allowing the computer to create all the inbetween frames is called which one of these?

A Twonking
B Honking
C Tweening
D Weening

ANSWERS

Questions A

▶ **TEXTBOOK PAGE 185**

1 One mark for each point to a maximum of two marks.
- The human eye sees an object after it has disappeared (1)
- This means that frames that change in an animation can appear smooth even though they are flicking from one to another (1)

2 One mark for each point to a maximum of two marks.
- A book that you flick through quickly (1)
- Each page contains an image that is slightly different from the previous one (1)
- Persistence of vision means the motion appears smooth (1)

3 One mark for each point to a maximum of three marks.
- A model is photographed and then moved slightly (1) and photographed again and so on (1)
- The photographs are combined (1)
- Tiny movements are joined together to show the model moving smoothly (1)

Questions B

▶ **TEXTBOOK PAGE 187**

1 (a) One mark for each point to a maximum of two marks.
  - A form of advertising you see on websites (1)
  - They are embedded into the website (1)
  - They provide a link to the advertiser's site (1)
 (b) One mark for:
  - So they can fit into a website design (1)
 (c) One mark for a reason such as:
  - They are distracting (1)
  - They can take a while to load, particularly if they include animations (1)

2 One mark for an advantage and one mark for a disadvantage.
Advantages of animation
- It can help explain a difficult concept (e.g., the greenhouse effect, the nitrogen cycle, etc.)
- It can be used to entertain young children
- It can attract users to a website
- It can make learning fun for young children
Disadvantages of animation
- Good animation can be expensive to produce
- It can distract users away from the content or the message being given
- On a website, it can take a while to load, which can put off some visitors to the website

Questions C

▶ **TEXTBOOK PAGE 191**

1 (a) One mark each for two of the following: png, cgm, gif, etc.
 (b) One mark for each point to a maximum of two marks similar to the following:
  - In vector animation the motion is controlled by vectors rather than pixels

- Vectors are changed by the use of mathematical equations
- In bitmap animation the arrangement of bits on the screen changes in some way and a new bitmap is produced

2 One mark for each point to a maximum of three marks such as:
- Several frames in an animation are superimposed over each other
- Allows the animator to see the frames before the frame they are producing next
- Allows them to check that the sequence of frames is correct
- Helps them decide what to draw next
- Enables them to produce frames that will produce smooth motion

3 (a) One mark for bitmap.
 (b) One mark for pixelation.

Test yourself

▶ **TEXTBOOK PAGE 192**

A Flip
B special effects
C Key
D stop motion
E Tweening
F storyboard
G mood board
H awareness

Examination style questions

▶ **TEXTBOOK PAGE 192**

1 One mark for each point to a maximum of four marks.
- When an object is viewed by the eye and it disappears
- The eye still sees it for a short amount of time
- This is called persistence of vision
- Use is made of this in animation
- To make the transition from one frame to another smooth

2 (a) One mark each for two points such as:
  - It is a visual representation of everything on the presentation or website (1)
  - It tells an animator the key frames in the animation (1)
  - It presents the story the multimedia product must tell (1)
 (b) One mark for one of the following:
  - It can make a subject come alive (1)
  - It will keep them interested in the topic (1)
  - It can present a story in a different way rather than reading about it in text (1)
 (c) One mark for one of the following:
  - It can distract from the content (1)
  - Not everything can be made fun or a game (1)
  - May put off some of the brighter children who may prefer to use their own imagination (1)

Worksheet: Animation anagrams

▶ **TEACHER'S RESOURCE GUIDE TOPIC 17 PAGE 118**

1 Persistence
2 Flip book
3 Stop motion
4 Key frame
5 Tweening
6 Virtual
7 Logo
8 Web banner
9 Folder tree
10 Storyboard

Multiple-choice questions

▶ **TEACHER'S RESOURCE GUIDE TOPIC 17 PAGE 123**

1B, 2A, 3D, 4B, 5D, 6B, 7A, 8B, 9D, 10C

Worksheet   pp. 196–200

Sound and music anagrams

Here are some words or phrases that have been jumbled up. The words are connected with Sound and music. Can you work out what they are? There is a clue to help you.

1 Woodland

   Hint: A music track obtained off the Internet.

   Answer: _____

2 Acorns dud

   Hint: You need one of these in your computer to play sound.

   Answer: _____

3 Niche promo

   Hint: The most popular input device for inputting sound.

   Answer: _____

4 Iconic region veto

   Hint: Recognizing spoken words.

   Answer: _____

5 Enact fire

   Hint: Musical Instrument Digital _____

   Answer: _____

6 Eureka plods

   Hint: Used to output sound.

   Answer: _____

7 Ale guano

   Hint: Type of wave or signal.

   Answer: _____

8 Tail dig

   Hint: Type of wave or signal.

   Answer: _____

9 Rec queens

   Hint: Hardware or software used to create and manage electronic music.

   Answer: _____

10 Ran toot

   Hint: A piece of software that allows you to compose your own music.

   Answer: _____

▶ Multiple-choice questions

pp. 196–200

1 Which one of the following statements is incorrect?

A An MP3 player plays music
B MP3 is a type of file used to store music
C MP3 is a type of file used for storing word-processed documents
D MP3 uses compression to enable more tracks to be stored

2 Which one of these is the input device used with a voice recognition system?

A A microphone
B A speaker
C A touchscreen
D A printer

3 Download means which one of these?

A Taking a file from a large computer/ server and loading it onto your own computer using the Internet
B Writing down instructions
C Storing a file on the Internet
D Creating a website

4 Which one of these is an output device?

A A keyboard
B A joystick
C Speakers
D A mouse

5 Here is a list of devices. How many of them are output devices?

Speakers   Headphones   Mouse
Scanner   Printer

A 2
B 3
C 4
D 1

6 Sound cards in a computer are used for which one of these purposes?

A Processing data to produce high quality sound
B Taking digital photographs
C Recording CDs
D Recording DVDs

7 Notators are best described as which one of these?

A Software to compose music
B A device to play CDs
C A screen
D A type of printer

8 Which one of these statements is incorrect?

A An iPod is an example of an MP3 player
B You can download music tracks as MP3 files using the Internet
C Downloading music off the Internet is always illegal
D You can pay to download music legally

9 A sound wave editor does which one of these?

A Allows you to print out sound
B Allows you to alter a recorded sound
C Allows you to play music CDs
D Allows you to word-process sound

10 Buying music from a site such as Amazon and transferring it directly to your home computer is called which one of these?

A Downloading
B Uploading
C Editing
D Compressing

ANSWERS

Questions A

▶ **TEXTBOOK PAGE 198**

1 (a) One mark for analogue
  (b) One mark for digital
  (c) One mark for analogue to digital converter
2 One mark each for two devices such as:
  • Headphones
  • Earphones/earpieces
  • Loudspeakers/speakers

Questions B

▶ **TEXTBOOK PAGE 200**

1 (a) One mark for each of two file formats such as:
  • wma (Windows Media Audio)
  • MP3
  • wav
  • qt (QuickTime)
  • MIDI
  (b) One mark for an explanation such as:
  • The file size is made smaller
  (c) One mark for one of the following:
  • Enables more music files to be stored on the media
  • Reduces the time needed to transfer the files over the Internet
2 (a) One mark for an explanation such as:
  • A file copied from a distant computer to the one you are working on
  (b) One mark for each point to a maximum of two marks.
  • The download can be obtained almost instantly
  • You can just download the tracks you want rather than the whole CD
  • The download is already in MP3 file format so no time wasted converting it
  (c) One mark for each point to a maximum of two marks.
  • Viruses may be introduced
  • Downloads may be illegal
  • You may want to use a CD player so you need to burn the tracks before use
  • You do not have all the notes that you sometimes get with a CD
  • You have nothing to sell if you get fed up with the music

Test yourself

▶ **TEXTBOOK PAGE 201**

A MP3
B sound card
C microphone
D loudspeakers
E analogue
F digital
G notator
H Sequencers
I wav
J wma

Examination style questions

▶ **TEXTBOOK PAGE 201**

1 (a) One mark each for two points.
  • A notator is a piece of software (1) that allows you to compose your own music (1) and you do this by entering notes into the computer (1)
  (b) One mark each for two points.
  • Sequencers are hardware or software (1) used to create and manage electronic music (1)
  • They include drum machines (1) and music workstations (1)
  (c) One mark each for two points.
  • Sound wave editors are software (1) that allows the editing of sound waves
  • Sound waves can be edited, cut, copied, pasted and have special effects added (1)
2 (a) One mark for one advantage:
  • File size is small (1)
  • More music tracks can be stored (1)
  One mark for one disadvantage:
  • Because of compression, some sound quality is lost
  • The file takes a little time to decode
  (b) (i) One mark for one advantage such as:
  • You do not need to buy the whole CD
  • You do not have to wait for a CD to be delivered
  • In a format players can use directly
  • Much wider choice of downloads compared to a music store
  (ii) One mark for one disadvantage such as:
  • You do not have a CD that you could sell at a car boot sale or on eBay
  • You have to enter payment details that could be stolen
  • You do not have the cover notes that come with a CD
  • Viruses could be downloaded with the music
3 (a) One mark to a maximum of four for points similar to the following:
  • By using the Internet music files can be used off websites if copyright permission allows
  • The development of removable storage media has meant that music files are easily transferred between devices
  • Compression techniques mean music files can be reduced in size so that more of them can be stored in the same place
  • Compression of files means that they are uploaded or downloaded using the Internet in a short period of time
  (b) One mark for an ethical issue and one mark for a legal issue.
  • Legal – file sharing sites encouraging users to share their music files with each other rather than buying them
  • Ethical – people loading digital music on many different devices that are used simultaneously against the licence agreement

Worksheet: Sound and music anagrams

▶ **TEACHER'S RESOURCE GUIDE TOPIC 18 PAGE 126**

1 Download
2 Sound card
3 Microphone
4 Voice recognition
5 Interface
6 Loudspeaker
7 Analogue
8 Digital
9 Sequencer
10 Notator

Multiple-choice questions

▶ **TEACHER'S RESOURCE GUIDE TOPIC 18 PAGE 127**

1C, 2A, 3A, 4C, 5B, 6A, 7A, 8C, 9B, 10A

▶ Worksheet   pp. 206–213

Networks anagrams

Here are some words or phrases that have been jumbled up. The words are connected with Networks. Can you work out what they are? There is a clue to help you.

1 Grin   *Hint: Type of network topology.*

Answer: _____

2 Tsar   *Hint: Type of network topology.*

Answer: _____

3 Sub   *Hint: Type of network topology.*

Answer: _____

4 Enter tin   *Hint: The largest network.*

Answer: _____

5 Rain tent   *Hint: Private network.*

Answer: _____

6 True or   *Hint: Device for joining networks.*

Answer: _____

7 Rent wok   *Hint: Group of computers able to communicate with each other.*

Answer: _____

8 Away get   *Hint: Use for connecting a LAN to a WAN.*

Answer: _____

9 Nil etc   *Hint: _____ server network.*

Answer: _____

10 Air do   *Hint: Type of signal used to send information.*

Answer: _____

▶ Multiple-choice questions

1 The way computers are connected in a network is called which one of these?

A Topology
B Ring
C Star
D Bus

2 The biggest network of computers in the world is called which one of these?

A Intranet
B Internet
C Extranet
D LAN

3 Devices that join several wired or wireless networks together are called which one of these

A WANs
B LANs
C Routers
D Hubs

4 The device/software that translates between two different kinds of computer networks (e.g., between a WAN and a LAN) is called which one of these?

A Gateway
B Subway
C Switch
D Hub

5 A computer used on its own without any connection (wireless or wire) to a network is called which of these?

A A networked computer
B A stand-alone computer
C A ring
D A bus

6 Intranets are very popular with small organizations.

Which of these statements about intranets is false?

A Intranets are private networks
B They can be used for sending internal mail
C They use the same network technology as the Internet
D Customers, suppliers and other trading partners are allowed access

7 Which one of these statements is false?

A The main feature of a WAN is that the hardware is spread over a wide geographical area
B With a WAN third party telecommunications equipment is used
C With a WAN the organization owns the communication equipment used
D WANs are spread over many buildings and sites

8 Which one of the following statements about networks is false?

A They allow resources to be shared
B Cables are always required between computers on the network
C The backing up of data is improved because it is often done centrally
D Networks are protected by usernames and passwords

9   **Which one of the following statements about extranets is true?**

A   An extranet does not use Internet technology

B   They are only used by employees of the organization

C   They can be used by customers, suppliers as well as employees of the organization

D   Extranets are only ever used inside the organization

10 **Which one of the following would you not find as part of a PoS terminal?**

A   A bar code reader

B   A chip and pin reader

C   A swipe card reader

D   An optical mark reader

ANSWERS

Questions A

▶ **TEXTBOOK PAGE 209**

1 One mark for local area network.

2 One mark for a definition similar to:
An arrangement of computers that are able to share data and resources

3 (a) One mark for each point to a maximum of two marks.
 • A single computer (1)
 • Not connected to other computers (1)
 • So is unable to share resources (1)
 • Unable to share files (1)

 (b) One mark for a difference such as:
 With a peer-to-peer network all the computers are of equal status whereas with client-server there is one more powerful computer in charge of the network

 (c) One mark for one point such as:
 • Client-server should be used when it is a larger network (1)
 • There is centralized storage of programs and data (1)
 • It is much easier to back up data using a client-server network (1)

4 (a) Any four features (one mark each) of peer-to-peer such as:
 • All computers in the network have the same status
 • All computers have access to each other's files provided file permissions allow
 • Very simple network to set up, which enables all computers to share resources
 • Limited security
 • All computers on the network act as clients as well as servers
 • There is no central server managing the network
 • Data can be replicated over several peers, which means the system is very robust
 • No centralized server means each peer is responsible for their own security which means that peer-to-peer networks are more susceptible to virus attacks

 (b) Any four features (one mark each) of client-server such as:
 • Servers provide centralized storage of data, installation of software, backup and security
 • The computers on the network are either servers or clients, not both
 • If the server goes down then any services it provides will be lost
 • Servers provide a centralized store of data which can be accessed by any computers on the network provided the permissions allow it
 • The client computers send requests to the server to use some of its services such as programs and data

5 Any two (one mark each for a named network and one mark for a correct diagram).
 • Ring
 • Bus
 • Star
 • Mesh

6 (a) One mark for shared resources and one mark for no connection.
 • Computers in a LAN are linked together (either by wires, fibre optic cable or wireless) and can share resources such as programs, files, printers, scanners, etc.
 • Stand-alone computers have no connection to other computers and can only use their own resources.

(b) Any two (one mark each) of the following:
 • Students can use any terminal – it does not matter where they sit, as the resources they can use will be the same
 • Software is standardized at each terminal
 • Central control of backup means that students are much less likely to lose their work
 • Students can communicate with other students on the LAN using instant messaging or email
 • Students can share files/data with each other, which is useful if they are doing group work
 • Important information/messages for students can be displayed when they log on to the network
 • Hardware resources such as scanners, printers, etc., can be shared

(c) Any two (one mark each) of the following:
 • If the server fails, then any data or programs stored on the server will be unavailable
 • There is a limited amount of storage given to each student on the network, which may restrict what they can do
 • If the network is being used for demanding applications, then it will slow down considerably
 • Time wasted by students forgetting their usernames and passwords
 • There are usually restrictions on the amount of printouts that students can produce over the network
 • Students are unable to customize their desktops and other software because each time the software is loaded it reverts back to a previous version
 • Students can waste time sending each other messages, and there is scope for online bullying

Questions B

▶ **TEXTBOOK PAGE 211**

1 One mark each for advantages/disadvantages to a maximum of four marks.
 • Do not need to sink wires (1)
 • No trailing network wires to trip over (1)
 • Wireless networks can be accessed anywhere in the building (1)
 • No cost of wires with a wireless network (1)
 • Wireless networks can be used outside (1)
 • Wireless networks can be hacked into (1)

2 One mark for each of three ways (maximum three):
 • Metal wires (1)
 • Fibre optic cable (1)
 • Wireless (1)

3 One mark for 'router'.

Questions C

▶ **TEXTBOOK PAGE 213**

1 One mark for each advantage to a maximum of three marks.
 • You can share hardware
 • Software can be installed in one place
 • Improved security
 • Speed – it is very quick to copy and transfer files
 • Cost as it is cheaper to buy network versions of software
 • Availability of email facilities
 • Access to a central store of data

2 (a) One mark for each of two advantages:
- Two people can access patient details at the same time
- Internal email can be sent
- Printers may be shared
- Easier to take backup copies
- All the computers can have access to the Internet
- It is easier to ensure the security of patient data

(b) One mark for each rule up to a maximum of four marks.
- Not to copy the data onto portable media without permission
- Not to leave their computer logged on unless they are there using it
- To change their passwords regularly
- To shred any printouts no longer needed
- Not to load any unauthorized software onto the computer, which could be a source of viruses

(c) One mark for one advantage such as:
- They can use the Internet to send emails to patients
- They can use the Internet to search for suppliers of goods and services
- They can use the Internet to research the latest developments in dentistry
- They can book conferences, trade fairs, etc.

One mark for one disadvantage such as:
- Possibility of hackers using the Internet to hack into patient files
- Staff could open file attachments to emails which contain viruses
- Staff could waste time surfing the Internet

3 One mark for each device (maximum three) such as:
- Printers
- Internet connection
- Database/files/file server
- Scanners
- Graph plotters

4 (a) One mark for each of two methods such as:
- Wireless/Bluetooth
- Fibre optic/glass fibre cables

(b) One mark for
- A computer which does not have a network connection
- A computer that is not connected to the Internet

(c) One mark for each of the following to a maximum of two marks.
- Network operating system/network software
- Firewall
- Modem (dialup or cable)
- Network interface card
- Metal wires/cables
- Hub
- Server
- Bridge
- Switch
- Router

Test yourself

▶ **TEXTBOOK PAGE 214**

A network
B LANs
C WANs
D peer-to-peer
E client-server
F topology
G bus
H ring
I star
J Internet
K router
L bridge

Examination style questions

▶ **TEXTBOOK PAGE 215**

1 (a) Two features (one mark each) such as:
- Only employees of the organization can access it
- Used within the organization
- Uses the same technology as the Internet
- Is a private network

(b) Two features (one mark each) such as:
- A private network
- Customers, suppliers and other trading partners can access but not others
- Uses the same technology as the Internet

2 (a) One mark for an answer similar to:
A series of computers that can communicate with each other and share resources.

(b) (i) One mark for:
Local area network

(ii) Two marks for an answer similar to:
A computer network confined to a single site/building, uses cable, wireless, infrared and microwave links which are usually owned by the organization

3 (a) One mark for Gateway.

(b) One mark for each difference to a maximum of two marks.
- WAN – uses third party communication systems
- WAN – spread over a wide geographical area
- LAN – confined to a single site or building
- LAN – the school would own the communications equipment
- WAN – used for large networks
- LAN – used for small networks

4 One mark for a brief statement of the advantages and one mark for further description or an example × 4.
- You can share hardware (1) – you can just have one printer and one scanner, as any of the computers connected to the network can use them (1)
- Software can be installed in one place (1) – you do not need to install software on each computer (1). This makes it faster to install and easier to maintain (1). If the software needs to be upgraded then this is much easier if only one copy is used (1)
- Improved security (1) – work can be saved on the network. The network manager will make sure that the work is backed up (1). Passwords make sure that other people cannot access your work unless you want them to (1)
- Speed (1) – it is very quick to copy and transfer files (1)
- Cost (1) – when software is bought, the school can buy network versions. These are much cheaper than buying a copy for each stand-alone computer (1)
- Email facilities (1) – any user of the network will be able to communicate using electronic mail (1)
- Access to a central store of data (1) – users will have access to centrally stored data (1)

5 (a) One mark each for two input devices such as:
- Bar code reader/laser scanner (1) – for the reading of bar codes on the goods so that a price and description are looked up (1)

- Touch screen (1) – so that goods can be bought by touching the screen (1)
- Magnetic strip reader (1) – for reading the data contained in a magnetic strip about customers on loyalty cards (1)
- Chip and pin reader (1) – used to read the payment details encrypted in the chip on a credit/debit card
- Keyboard (1) – used for the manual input of item numbers and codes when bar codes and other methods fail to work (1)

(b) One mark for the name of the system and one mark for the description × 2.
- Payment systems (1) – where the customer can pay using credit/debit card (1)
- Loyalty card systems (1) – where customers are given loyalty points according to how much they spend (1)
- Accounts systems (1) – where the money coming into the shop is accounted for (1)
- Automatic stock control systems (1) – the system knows what has been sold so that it can automatically reorder more once the stock falls below a certain amount (1)

Worksheet: Networks anagrams

▶ **TEACHER'S RESOURCE GUIDE TOPIC 19 PAGE 130**

1 Ring
2 Star
3 Bus
4 Internet
5 Intranet
6 Router
7 Network
8 Gateway
9 Client
10 Radio

Multiple-choice questions

▶ **TEACHER'S RESOURCE GUIDE TOPIC 19 PAGE 131**

1A, 2B, 3C, 4A, 5B, 6D, 7C, 8B, 9C, 10D

▶ Worksheet

pp. 220–223

HCI anagrams

Here are some words or phrases that have been jumbled up. The words are connected with Human-computer interfaces. Can you work out what they are? There is a clue to help you.

1 A regiments typos   *Hint: The software used to control the hardware directly.*

Answer: _____

2 Opticians pal   *Hint: Type of software used to perform a particular job.*

Answer: _____

3 Wind sow   *Hint: Brand of operating system.*

Answer: _____

4 Award her   *Hint: The physical components of a computer system.*

Answer: _____

5 Fear twos   *Hint: Another name for programs.*

Answer: _____

6 Proteins   *Hint: The 'P' in WIMP.*

Answer: _____

7 Sonic   *Hint: Small pictures you click on.*

Answer: _____

8 Dins wow   *Hint: The 'W' in WIMP.*

Answer: _____

9 A larch pig   *Hint: A type of user interface.*

Answer: _____

10 Orbits mice   *Hint: Makes use of features of the human body that are unique.*

Answer: _____

▶ Multiple-choice questions pp. 220–223

1 Which one of the following is not performed by an operating system?

A Allocating space for files on a disk
B Issuing an instruction to the printer to start printing
C Managing the flow of data from the keyboard
D Searching for a record in a database

2 Using the Windows operating system, you can print out a large amount of material while you are doing some word processing. This is called which of the following?

A Transaction processing
B Batch processing
C Multitasking
D Spellchecking

3 GUI stands for which of these?

A Geographical user information
B Great user interface
C Graphical user interface
D Graphical user input

4 Windows is an operating system. Which one of the following best describes the type of user interface it uses?

A GUI
B Command line
C Robot driven
D Optical character recognition

5 Many devices now use a touch screen interface.

Which one of these is *not* a reason why touch screens are popular?

A They are very easy for members of the public to use
B They allow portable devices to be made small
C You can use a GUI with a touch screen
D Touch screens are more accurate than other types of interface

6 Why are graphical user interface (GUI) systems so popular?

A They speed up processing
B They save space in the memory
C They make computers easier to use
D They reduce hardware costs

7 Which one of the following is *not* a trade name for a type of systems software?

A UNIX
B Linux
C Windows
D Office

8 Which one of the following best describes the meaning of the word interface?

A The method used by a computer to communicate with its user
B An input device such as a mouse
C A type of systems software
D A device used to access the Internet

▶ Multiple-choice questions (continued)

pp. 220–223

9 **Which one of the following would you *not* find as part of a graphical user interface?**

A Windows
B Icons
C Menus
D Command line

10 **The type of interface where spoken language is used to communicate with the computer is called which one of these?**

A Spoken language interface
B Natural language interface
C Thought control
D Voice recognition

ANSWERS

Questions A

▶ **TEXTBOOK PAGE 221**

1 One mark for each way to a maximum of two marks.
- They can alter the screen resolution
- They can alter the brightness and contrast of the screen
- They can alter the size of the icons
- They can adjust the way the mouse works
- Etc.

2 (a) Two marks allocated as follows:
Software (1) that controls the operation of the hardware directly (1)
(b) One mark each for any three of the following:
- Manages and controls any peripheral devices that are attached to the computer
- Provides a user interface that makes it easy for the user to load programs, search for files, copy files, etc.
- Hides the complexity of the hardware from the user
- Deals with any errors that occur while the computer is working on tasks
- Provides the interface between the application packages being run and the hardware
- Allows new hardware or software to be installed using installation programs
- Contains various utilities such as disk formatter, virus checking, encryption, etc.
- Deals with system security
(c) One mark for one of the following:
- UNIX
- LINUX
- MAC OS
- DOS
- SUN

Questions B

▶ **TEXTBOOK PAGE 223**

1 One mark for the feature and other mark for the example × 2:
- You simply talk to the software and tell it what to do using words such as print and save
- You can issue instructions to the computer using normal language, e.g. find me the document called Letter to the headmistress 1 June 2011
- You can ask a question simply by speaking directly into the microphone, for example 'What is the capital of Chile?'

2 (a) Two marks for a definition similar to this with two points.
Software that controls the hardware of a computer and used to run the applications software. Operating systems control the handling of input, output, etc.
(b) One mark for the answer: Graphical user interface
(c) One mark for a definition: The user has to type in instructions in a certain language or from a list of commands for a command line interface
(d) One mark for one of these two reasons:
- New users do not have to remember a set of commands or how they must be constructed
- Experienced users will prefer to type in commands to do things because it is faster

3 (a) One mark each for two points such as:
- Rather than use a mouse and keyboard (1) you simply touch items on the GUI on the screen (1)

- You can key in data (1) by using a touch sensitive keyboard that appears on the screen (1)
- You can move items on the screen using your fingers (1)
- You can size images on the screen using your fingers (1)
- You can select files simply by touching them (1)
(b) One mark for one of the following (it must be clear where the touch aspect comes in):
- Mobile telephone (e.g. i-Phone) being used to search the Internet by touching on website links
- Tablet PC being used when standing up to take a school register by touching next to student names
- An MP3 player being used to select songs to make up a play list by touching the songs and moving your finger to the list

Test yourself

▶ **TEXTBOOK PAGE 224**

A hardware, system
B printers
C errors
D storage
E recognizes
F interface
G line
H menu-driven
I GUI
J voice

Examination style questions

▶ **TEXTBOOK PAGE 225**

1 One mark for each correct answer.
B Supervising the running of other programs
D Transferring data between memory and the hard drive
E Maximizing the use of the computer's memory
2 One mark for each interface up to a maximum of three marks.
- GUI
- Command line/command driven
- Voice driven
- Menu/dialogue boxes
- Touch sensitive
- Biometrics
3 One mark for each correctly marked tick.

	True	False
An operating system is always software	√	
Operating systems supervise the running of other software	√	
Operating systems must be loaded before the computer can do a useful job	√	
Operating systems handle outputs but not inputs		√

4 (a) One mark for each feature:
- WIMP (only allow one mark if on own without Windows, Icons, etc.)
- Windows
- Icons

- Menus
- Pointers
- Office assistant
- Online tutorials
- Online help
- Customized desktops

(b) (i) One mark each for two different interfaces such as:
- Command line/command driven
- Voice driven
- Menu/dialogue boxes
- Touch sensitive
- Biometrics

(ii) One mark for correct advantage which must relate to answer in part (i).
- Command line – faster for an experienced user to achieve the same result as someone who works through all the menus
- Voice driven – easiest interface to use and you can use spoken commands
- Menu/dialogue boxes – ideal for when the user has to enter information such as personal details for an online order
- Touch sensitive – do not need knowledge of how to use a keyboard
- Biometrics – ideal as the user has only to be present themselves for them to be recognized by a system.

5 One mark for each correct tick. Subtract one mark for each wrong tick but do not allow marks to fall below zero.

Task	Performed by the operating system
Searching for a record in a database	
Allocating space for files on the disk drive	√
Issuing an instruction to the printer to start printing	√
Formatting text in a word-processed document	
Managing the flow of data from a keyboard	√
Controlling the security of a system	√
Altering the margins in a package	

Worksheet: HCI anagrams

▶ **TEACHER'S RESOURCE GUIDE TOPIC 20 PAGE 136**

1 Operating system
2 Applications
3 Windows
4 Hardware
5 Software
6 Pointers
7 Icons
8 Windows
9 Graphical
10 Biometrics

Multiple-choice questions

▶ **TEACHER'S RESOURCE GUIDE TOPIC 20 PAGE 137**

1D, 2C, 3C, 4A, 5D, 6C, 7D, 8A, 9D, 10D

▶ Worksheet

pp. 230–242

Organizations anagrams

Here are some words or phrases that have been jumbled up. The words are connected with Organizations. Can you work out what they are? There is a clue to help you.

1 Come rec me   *Hint: Using the Internet to conduct business.*

   Answer: _____

2 Carat update   *Hint: How the data gets into the computer system.*

   Answer: _____

3 Vial us   *Hint: Check performed by looking.*

   Answer: _____

4 Ale timer   *Hint: Processing occurs immediately.*

   Answer: _____

5 China tops   *Hint: Another name for an ATM.*

   Answer: _____

6 Ray poll   *Hint: Process of paying staff.*

   Answer: _____

7 Fade beck   *Hint: Where the output from the system directly affects the input.*

   Answer: _____

8 Ibis con   *Hint: Apply biological science to robotics.*

   Answer: _____

9 Rob to   *Hint: Mechanical device that can be programmed to perform a sequence of actions.*

   Answer: _____

10 Sexy tempters   *Hint: System used to make decisions.*

   Answer: _____

▶ Activity   pp. 236–237

Researching the use of robots

For this activity you have to use the Internet for research to find out about as many different uses for robots as you can.

You then have to produce a document that contains a picture of the robot along with a brief explanation as to how it is used.

To help you get the idea, one has been done for you.

1

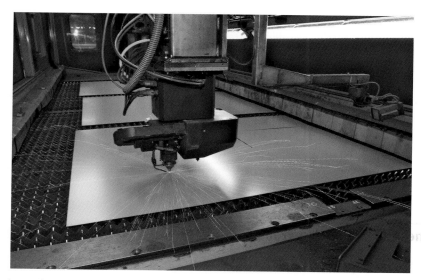

This is a robot that uses laser to cut patterns in sheet metal. These sheets are then shaped to form the panels for car bodies. The panels are then welded together also by a robot.

▶ Multiple-choice questions | pp. 230–242

1 Which method is used to input data from bank cheques?

A MICR
B OMR
C OCR
D Bar coding

2 Multiple choice answer sheets use OMR. The sheets are collected together and processed in one go. This is an example of which one of the following?

A Real-time processing
B Real-time (transaction) processing
C Batch processing
D Now and again processing

3 Which of these is the output from a payroll system?

A Printed time sheets
B Printed pay slips
C Bills
D Word-processed documents

4 A school enters details from a form filled in by parents when a new entrant joins the school. What would be a suitable method of verification?

A Range checks
B Proof reading (visual checks)
C Data type checks
D Check digits

5 OMR is *least* likely to be used as an input device in which one of the following applications?

A For recording lottery ticket numbers
B For marking multiple-choice answer sheets
C School registers
D Data logging

6 Which one of the following is *not* an advantage of online banking?

A Availability of services 24/7, 365 days per year
B Faster then queuing up in a bank
C There is a danger of identity theft
D You do not have to waste time travelling to banks

7 A large amount of typed text in a book needs to be digitized so that it can be input into a word-processor. Which of the following is the fastest and easiest method of entering this data?

A Scanning the text and then using OCR software
B Using MICR
C Typing it in using a keyboard
D Using OMR

8 What does OCR stand for?

A Ordinary character recognition
B Optical character recognition
C Optical combination recognition
D Optical combination reader

9 Which of the following is a suitable application for OCR?

A The processing of bank cheques
B The reading of number plates at a port
C The recording of numbers on a lottery ticket
D The recording of weather data from a remote weather station

10 Which one of these are programs that replicate a human expert on a specific subject?

A Database software
B Expert systems
C Word-processing software
D Operating systems software

ANSWERS

Questions A

► TEXTBOOK PAGE 231

1 (a) One mark for one of the following:
- They may be hacked into and the card details used fraudulently
- They may be a victim of identity theft

(b) One mark each for two of the following:
- Encrypt the banking details
- Use a secure connection between the customer and the store
- Ensure their own staff cannot view credit card details

(c) One mark for:
- Check that all the links work properly – with bogus sites only part of the site usually works properly
- Check to see if there are reviews from other buyers
- Ring the phone number if there is one
- Check there is an address

2 (a) One mark each for two points.
- Use the mouse to make selections/adding items to shopping trolley/basket
- Enter personal details using a keyboard

(b) One mark for each method up to a maximum of two marks.
- Visual check
- Presence check
- Range check
- Etc.

(c) One mark for one method.
- Email order confirmation on screen
- Print out of order/hard copy

Questions B

► TEXTBOOK PAGE 233

1 (a) One mark for each of the following:
- Credit cards
- Debit cards

(b) One mark for each point to a maximum of four marks.
- To combat fraud (1)
- People could use the card if they could forge the signature on them (1)
- It does not rely on a signature being compared (1)
- There is a number encrypted in the chip (1)
- The user needs to be able to enter this PIN to use the card at a store (1)
- Only the user of the card would know this number (1)
- Uses a personal identification number to authenticate the card user (1)
- This system reduces the fraudulent use of cards (1)
- It is much harder to use a stolen card (1)

2 (a) One mark for two of the following such as:
- The card could be stolen and used to buy goods or services
- The card details could be obtained and used to make purchases over the Internet where you do not need the actual card

(b) One mark for one of the following:
- Use a chip and pin card
- Shred any details containing your name, address, credit card details, etc.
- Ensure you use virus checkers that will check for programs that record your credit card details
- Ensure sites use encryption for card details

Questions C

► TEXTBOOK PAGE 235

1 (a) One mark for one of the following points:
- Working out the pay for each employee
- Calculating wages
- Working out deductions (tax, National Insurance, etc.)

(b) (i) One mark each for two methods such as:
- Keyboarding/typing in the details
- Use OMR
- Use OCR
- Voice recognition
- Automatic data capture (e.g., using data directly from a clocking in/out machine)

(ii) One mark for:
- Payslip

2 (a) One mark for: Optical mark recognition (OMR).

(b) One mark for one of the following:
- The data is captured quickly
- No need to pay someone to type the data in
- More accurate than typing

(c) One mark for: Batch processing.
One mark for: All the inputs are grouped/batched together and processed in one go

Questions D

► TEXTBOOK PAGE 237

1 One mark each for two advantages such as:
- Safer in certain environments – e.g., paint spraying where fumes are dangerous
- Lower cost – you do not have to pay robots wages
- Better quality – there is no human error
- Faster – the robot can complete more work in the same time as it does not get tired
- Can work 24/7

2 One mark for each point to a maximum of two marks.
- A robot is a device that can be programmed (1) to perform a sequence of actions (1)
- Robots can be re-programmed (1) with a new set of instructions so that they are able to carry out a completely different task (1)

Questions E

► TEXTBOOK PAGE 239

1 (a) One mark for each point to a maximum of two marks.
An expert system is an ICT system that uses artificial intelligence (1) to make decisions based on data supplied in the form of answers to questions (1). This means that the system is able to respond in the way that a human expert (1) in the field would to come to a conclusion (1)

(b) Any two (one mark each) from the following:
- Knowledge base
- Inference engine
- User interface

(c) One mark for one of the following:
- More accurate diagnosis
- Fewer mistakes as computers do not forget things
- Cheaper than employing a consultant or expert

(d) One mark for one of the following:
- Can check what they think with what the expert system thinks/get second opinion
- Patient may answer questions more truthfully if they are asked the questions by a computer

(e) One mark for one of the following:
- Lacks common sense
- Lacks senses (e.g., can't tell pain from patient's body language)
- Only as good as the person who set it up

2 (a) One mark each to a maximum of three for:
- Knowledge base
- Inference engine
- User interface

(b) One mark each to a maximum of two marks for:
- Leaves doctors/specialists more time to concentrate on serious cases
- The knowledge base can be kept more up-to-date
- Ordinary doctors can use the system to make an expert diagnosis without needing to contact a specialist
- There is faster diagnosis for patients, so patients get better quicker
- It is cheaper to use the expert system than train doctors in the specialist area
- A human may forget to consider a certain fact but the expert system will consider all the facts to arrive at a correct diagnosis

Questions F

▶ **TEXTBOOK PAGE 242**

1 One mark for a statement of the problem and one mark for further amplification or an example × 2.
- Hacking (1) – people can access information using the Internet (1)
- The introduction of viruses (1) – users may download software off the Internet that contains viruses (1)
- People viewing personal information (1) – when the person using a computer leaves their desk (1)

2 (a) One mark for each point to a maximum of two marks:
- Take regular backups
- Use physical security
- Keyboard locks
- Computers attached to desks to prevent being stolen
- To not allow users to insert removable media
- Keypads to prevent access to rooms

(b) One mark for each point to a maximum of two marks.
- Biometric methods (e.g., fingerprinting/retina scanning) to prevent unauthorized access to room/computers
- Use usernames and passwords to restrict access
- Use access rights, which prevents some users being able to access certain files

3 (a) Two marks allocated as follows:
- Identifies a particular user to the network (1) so that certain access rights can be given to the user (1)

(b) Two marks allocated as follows:
- So that the system can determine if the person is the correct person (1) for the username or someone who should be denied access to the network (1)

(c) Two marks allocated as follows:
- The scrambling of data (1) before it is transmitted over a communication channel or stored on media (1)

(d) One mark each for two points to a maximum of two marks.
- Keeps details of user accessing certain files (1)
- Keeps details of the changes made by the user (1)
- Used to provide evidence in cases of illegal access or fraud (1)
- Acts as a deterrent to others as the system is recording their actions (1)

(e) One mark each for two points to a maximum of two marks.
- Hardware or software (1) used to prevent illegal access using the Internet (1)

Test yourself

▶ **TEXTBOOK PAGE 243**

A Internet
B debit, hackers
C encrypted
D payroll
E control
F intelligence
G expert system
H feedback
I sensors

Examination style questions

▶ **TEXTBOOK PAGE 243**

1 (a) Three items (one mark each) such as:
- Card number
- Start date
- Expiry date

(b) (i) One mark for two advantages such as:
- Can use a cash point 24/7
- Quicker than waiting in a queue
- Often in places you have to visit anyway such as garages/shops
- Can park near when less busy

(ii) One mark each for two of the following:
- Can deposit cash
- Can change your PIN
- Can check a balance

2 (a) One mark for each service up to a maximum of three marks:
- View bank statements
- Transfer money between accounts
- Make payments for bills
- Apply for loans

(b) One mark for each up to a maximum of two marks:
- Worry about inputting the wrong data
- Worry about hackers accessing their banking details
- Worry about others using their account fraudulently

(c) One mark for one of the following:
- Worry about inputting the wrong data – bank can explain that range checks are used to check that huge amounts are not moved betweens accounts by mistake
- Worry about hackers accessing their banking details – explain how banking details are encrypted when passing between banks and customers
- Worry about others using their account fraudulently – explain how firewalls are used to keep personal details secure

Worksheet: Organizations anagrams

▶ **TEACHER'S RESOURCE GUIDE TOPIC 21 PAGE 141**

1 E-commerce
2 Data capture
3 Visual
4 Real time
5 Cash point
6 Payroll
7 Feedback
8 Bionics
9 Robot
10 Expert system

Multiple-choice questions

▶ **TEACHER'S RESOURCE GUIDE TOPIC 21 PAGE 143**

1A, 2C, 3B, 4B, 5D, 6C, 7A, 8B, 9B, 10B

▶ **Activity**   pp. 250–252

Teleworking would you like it or not?

You have an ordinary office job and your boss has asked you whether you would like to telework. Write a short paragraph of text to explain whether you would prefer to telework or not. In this piece, you will need to explain the reasons for your decision.

▶ Worksheet 1 | pp. 248–254

Social and environmental impact anagrams

Here are some words or phrases that have been jumbled up. The words are connected with Social and environmental impact. Can you work out what they are? There is a clue to help you.

1 Be crime cry

Hint: Crime committed using computers.

Answer: _____

2 Sealed hippo

Hint: People who groom young children using the Internet.

Answer: _____

3 Coke I so

Hint: Record details of the websites you have visited.

Answer: _____

4 Flicker ling

Hint: Job that has disappeared due to introduction of computers.

Answer: _____

5 Trainer

Hint: What you must do if your job changes.

Answer: _____

6 Ogre twinkle

Hint: Working from home using ICT equipment and telecommunications.

Answer: _____

7 Conference voiding

Hint: Face-to-face meetings to be conducted without the participants being in the same room or even the same geographical area.

Answer: _____

8 Dictators sin

Hint: You may have these if you work from home.

Answer: _____

9 Android icebox

Hint: Computer manufacture produces this gas.

Answer: _____

10 Cycle ring

Hint: Important to do this to reduce the carbon footprint.

Answer: _____

▶ **Worksheet 2** | pp. 248–254

Has the use of ICT had a positive or negative impact?

Some ICT developments have had positive effects on our lives while others have produced negative effects. Here are some statements and you have to decide whether they are positive or negative by completing the boxes in the following table.

Comments about ICT	Positive or negative?
It is very hard to keep your personal life private.	
New problems have been created such as cyberbullying.	
People are worried about having their identity stolen.	
Your personal life is no longer your own.	
Communication, wherever you are, is easier.	
Widens the gap between the haves and the have-nots.	
Creates a new group of ICT-related crimes.	
There are health problems associated with working with ICT equipment.	
Allows disabled people to work.	
Some employees are able to work from home.	
Using the Internet to shop means that you have a much greater choice of products and services to choose from.	
Using ICT can be very stressful.	
Mobile phones allow communication between people on the move (taxi drivers, reps, etc.).	
More realistic computer games are available that are more fun.	
Paying for goods is much faster using ICT.	
Mobile phones are useful in an emergency.	
You can use the Internet for research and this saves a trip to the library.	

▶ Worksheet 3 pp. 250–251

The way ICT has changed or even eliminated some jobs

Some jobs have been eliminated by ICT developments, others have been created, whilst other jobs have been changed. There are some jobs that have not been affected at all by ICT developments.

Here are some jobs. For each job, state with a reason whether the job has been **eliminated**, **created**, **changed** or **unaffected** by ICT developments.

(a) Call-centre work   _____

(b) Website designer   _____

(c) Selling mobile telephones   _____

(d) Filing clerk   _____

(e) Typewriter repair person   _____

(f) Secretary   _____

(g) Painter and decorator   _____

(h) Doctor   _____

(i) Teacher   _____

(j) Computer programmer   _____

(k) Writer   _____

▶ Multiple-choice questions

pp. 248–254

1 **Online shopping has become very popular. This may cause social problems.**

   Which one of these is a social problem caused by online shopping?

   A High street shops closing owing to not being able to compete with online stores
   B People having fewer goods to choose from
   C Not being able to return goods easily
   D Goods being sent from anywhere in the world

2 **The use of credit/debit cards for online purchases may alienate certain groups of society. Which one of the following groups is the most likely to be alienated?**

   A Retired people
   B Young professionals
   C The unemployed
   D Young adults

3 **Globalization is one consequence to society that the use of ICT brings. Globalization means which one of the following?**

   A Using ICT all around the world
   B Making countries less separate by the removal of economic and cultural barriers
   C Using the Internet to conduct business
   D All countries in the world having the same ICT laws

4 **Which one of these is a downside of globalization to society?**

   A Countries can lose their separate cultural identity
   B People have access to the same brands all around the world
   C Communication between all countries is made easier
   D It is more difficult for people to use computers

5 **The erosion of privacy is a major issue in society.**

   Which of the following systems causes major privacy issues?

   A The storing of credit card details by credit card companies
   B The use of CCTV cameras in conjunction with computers and face recognition software
   C The storing of names and addresses for mail shots
   D The storing of medical records by hospitals

6 **Teleworking means that many people can now work from home.**

   Which of the following is *not* a benefit to the individual in working from home?

   A People can fit work more around their family commitments
   B People are able to work longer hours
   C People can sometimes choose their own hours of work
   D People can live wherever they like

▶ **Multiple-choice questions**
(continued)

pp. 248–254

7 Older retired users are major users of ICT systems.

Which one of the following is *not* an important social advantage for these users?

A They can shop from home and remain independent

B They can keep in touch with family and friends cheaply by using Internet telephone calls

C They can use social networking sites to keep in touch with friends and make new ones

D They can run up gambling debts on the many online gaming sites

8 Which of the following is a disadvantage of teleworking for an employee?

A You do not have to commute to work

B There is less social interaction with other people

C You can fit in work with social arrangements

D There are no travelling costs

9 ICT systems have changed the way many people work and their work patterns.

Which of the following is not a social consequence of this?

A Fewer workstations needed

B More flexible working hours needed

C The ability to work from home

D Increased stress caused by the continual need to learn new things

10 Which one of the following statements is wrong?

A With the use of the ICT there is more part-time work

B The introduction of ICT has always led to job losses

C ICT can enable firms to become more profitable and take more staff on

D Many ICT systems are used 24/7

ANSWERS

Questions A

▶ TEXTBOOK PAGE 252

1 (a) Two jobs (one mark each) such as:
- Filing clerk
- Typist
- Welder
- Paint sprayer in a car factory
- Packers
- Stock takers
- Shop assistants
- Post clerk

(b) Any two jobs that have an obvious ICT connection such as:
- Managers
- Shop checkout staff
- Doctor
- Etc.

(c) One job for one mark such as:
- Call centre staff
- Telephone help-line staff
- Online bank advisor
- Airline booking clerk
- Telephone marketing staff

2 (a) Three jobs (one mark each) such as:
- Network managers
- Website designers
- Development staff/programmers/systems analysts
- Computer sales staff
- ICT repair staff/engineers

(b) One mark each for two points such as:
- New ICT systems are being introduced all the time (1)
- The technology is constantly changing (1)
- New hardware and software are used (1)
- Staff need to know how to work with these new systems (1)

3 (a) One mark for each point to a maximum of three marks:
- Using ICT equipment (1)
- And networking/telecommunications equipment (1)
- And online databases (1)
- To work from home (1)

(b) Two advantages (must be to the employer) for one mark each such as:
- Smaller offices needed
- Fewer backup staff such as caretakers needed
- Staff less likely to take time off sick
- Reduced office overheads (e.g. gas, electric, etc.)
- Staff more amenable to working flexible hours
- Less office furniture needed

(c) Two disadvantages (must be to the employer) for one mark each such as:
- Change to the structure of the organization may be needed
- Harder for managers to manage
- Increased security risk as computers are not located in one place
- More difficult to hold meetings
- Have to pay for equipment

Questions B

▶ TEXTBOOK PAGE 254

1 (a) One mark for each point to a maximum of two marks.
- Allows face-to-face meetings (1)
- To be conducted virtually (i.e., without the people being at the same place) (1)
- People can see the other people at the meeting on a screen (1)
- They can chat to them using a microphone (1)
- The can swap electronic documents and other files electronically (1)

(b) One mark for each of two items of equipment such as:
- Webcam/camera
- Microphone
- Broadband link
- Videoconferencing software
- Modem to connect to the Internet

(c) One mark for each advantage/disadvantage to two marks.

Advantages
- No time spent travelling
- No travel and accommodation costs
- More family friendly as do not need to spend time away from home
- Less stress as travelling is often stressful
- Much greener
- Does not clog roads up with people travelling to and from meetings
- Etc.

Disadvantages
- Products may need to be passed around – can't do this
- Sometimes the picture quality is poor
- People sometimes like to travel to new places
- Cost of the videoconferencing equipment can be high

2 One mark for each of two points, for example:
- Poor people may not have a credit or debit card (1)
- Because they are unemployed (1)
- So they cannot take advantage of cheap goods or services on the Internet (1)

Test yourself

▶ TEXTBOOK PAGE 255

A Internet
B social
C political
D moral
E Teleworking
F commitments
G distractions
H Videoconferencing
I rich
J power

Topic 22 Social and environmental impact

Examination style questions

▶ TEXTBOOK PAGE 255

1 One mark for each change to a maximum of three marks such as:
   - May have to take on many different types of role (1)
   - Constant need to retrain to take advantage of new technology (1)
   - May have to work more flexible hours (1)
   - Greater availability of part-time work (1)
   - May have the opportunity to telework (1)
   - Greater possibility of shift work (1)

2 One mark for each of two advantages such as:
   - No time wasted commuting
   - You can sometimes work your own hours
   - No expenses for travelling to work
   - You can live wherever you want
   - Ideal for disabled people
   - Less stress
   - You can fit work around family commitments

   One mark for each of two disadvantages such as:
   - Home costs such as heating and lighting increase
   - It may be isolating to work this way
   - Boundary between work and home is lost
   - May not be space or a quiet place in your house
   - No workmates to socialize with
   - May get disturbed by others in the house

3 One mark each for two suitable jobs such as:
   - Call centre staff
   - Telephone help-line staff
   - Online bank advisor
   - Airline booking clerk
   - Telephone marketing staff

4 One mark for each of three points, which must be in correctly structured sentences.
   - Robots are used to assemble engine components in cars (1)
   - The robots can be used to weld panels together (1)
   - The robots can be programmed to spray paint the cars (1)
   - They are cheaper and able to work 24/7 (1)

Activity: Teleworking would your like or not?

▶ TEACHER'S RESOURCE GUIDE TOPIC 22 PAGE 147

The best way to answer this is to look at the comments made by actual teleworkers.
Here are some comments from teleworkers:
'I find that there are too many distractions working at home.'
'It is harder to cut myself off from my work since work life and home life are intermingled.'
'I find that I am rarely sick because I no longer pick up all those bugs that go around the office.'
'I find working from home less stressful because I do not get caught up in traffic jams.'
'I have young children which I look after on my own. I can do the work at night when they are asleep. If I did not telework, I would not be able to work.'
'The climate is changing. Global warming is causing floods in many countries. I think that we should take steps to use our cars less. Teleworking is an answer.'
'Teleworking is not for me because I like to meet and interact with people.'

'I am severely disabled so it is hard for me to travel. Many organizations do not have ramps or lifts. Telecommuting is ideal for me.'
'I will lose out on promotion because my boss will not be aware how hard I am working.'
'I only have a small house and there is no real place for me to work.'

Worksheet 1: Social and environmental impact anagrams

▶ TEACHER'S RESOURCE GUIDE TOPIC 22 PAGE 148

1 Cybercrime
2 Paedophiles
3 Cookies
4 Filing clerk
5 Retrain
6 Teleworking
7 Videoconferencing
8 Distractions
9 Carbon dioxide
10 Recycling

Worksheet 2: Has the use of ICT had a positive or negative impact?

▶ TEACHER'S RESOURCE GUIDE TOPIC 22 PAGE 149

Comments about ICT	Positive or negative?
It is very hard to keep your personal life private.	Negative
New problems have been created such as cyberbullying.	Negative
People are worried about having their identity stolen.	Negative
Your personal life is no longer your own.	Negative
Communication, wherever you are, is easier.	Positive
Widens the gap between the haves and the have-nots.	Negative
Creates a new group of ICT-related crimes.	Negative
There are health problems associated with working with ICT equipment.	Negative
Allows disabled people to work.	Positive
Some employees are able to work from home.	Positive
Using the Internet to shop means that you have a much greater choice of products and services to choose from.	Positive
Using ICT can be very stressful.	Negative
Mobile phones allow communication between people on the move (taxi drivers, reps, etc.).	Positive
More realistic computer games are available that are more fun.	Positive
Paying for goods is much faster using ICT.	Positive
Mobile phones are useful in an emergency.	Positive
You can use the Internet for research and this saves a trip to the library.	Positive

Worksheet 3: The way ICT has changed or even eliminated some jobs

▶ **TEACHER'S RESOURCE GUIDE TOPIC 22 PAGE 150**

(a) Created
(b) Created
(c) Created
(d) Eliminated
(e) Eliminated
(f) Changed
(g) Unaffected
(h) Changed
(i) Changed
(j) Created
(k) Changed

Multiple-choice questions

▶ **TEACHER'S RESOURCE GUIDE TOPIC 22 PAGE 151**

1A, 2C, 3B, 4A, 5B, 6B, 7D, 8B, 9A, 10B

▶ Worksheet

pp. 260–264

Legal and ethical issues anagrams

Here are some words or phrases that have been jumbled up. The words are connected with Legal and ethical issues. Can you work out what they are? There is a clue to help you.

1 Contradict a teapot   *Hint: The law that protects our personal data.*

Answer: _____

2 Vary pic   *Hint: Keeping information about us private.*

Answer: _____

3 Parental soda   *Hint: Data about us.*

Answer: _____

4 A tad subject   *Hint: The person that personal data is about.*

Answer: _____

5 Nag hick   *Hint: The process of gaining illegal access to an ICT system.*

Answer: _____

6 Chirpy got   *Hint: All original works such as music are protected by this.*

Answer: _____

7 Rap icy   *Hint: Name for illegal copying.*

Answer: _____

8 Nuclear evils   *Hint: Snooping on someone.*

Answer: _____

9 Pencil rips   *Hint: There are eight of these in the Data Protection Act.*

Answer: _____

10 Acute car   *Hint: Personal data should be .... and up to date.*

Answer: _____

► Activity   pp. 260–264

Producing a newspaper article on new crimes created by ICT

You have been asked to produce a newspaper article for a local newspaper on new crimes created by the use of ICT.

You will have to do quite a bit of research finding out about these crimes.

Where do you start?

Here are some information sources you can start with:

Online newspapers:
  http://news.bbc.co.uk/
  http://www.guardian.co.uk/
  http://www.telegraph.co.uk/
  http://www.timesonline.co.uk/tol/news/

Articles on the Internet: use search engines with key words to find suitable information.

▶ Multiple-choice questions

pp. 260–264

1 What is the name of the law that makes hacking into a computer system illegal?

A Copyright, Designs and Patents Act 1988
B Data Protection Act 1998
C Computer Misuse Act 1990
D Freedom of Information Act 2005

2 Which one of the following statements is true?

A Organizations are never allowed to pass personal data to another organization
B If personal data is found to be incorrect, the data subject has the right to have it corrected
C You cannot consent to allowing your personal details to be processed and passed to others
D Religious beliefs are not classed as personal data

3 Which of these is an offence under The Computer Misuse Act 1990?

A Misusing personal data
B Hacking into a computer system
C Processing personal data
D Running purchased software in breach of the software licence

4 What is the name of the act that covers illegal copying of software?

A Computer Misuse Act 1990
B Health and Safety at Work Act 1974
C Freedom of Information Act 2005
D Copyright, Designs and Patents Act 1988

5 There are some exemptions from notification under the Data Protection Act 1998. Which one of the following is *not* a valid exemption?

A Where data is being held in connection with personal, family or household affairs or for recreational use
B Where data is used for preparing the text of documents
C Where the data is being held in the interests of national security
D Where personal data is held by a government department

6 Which of these is the correct definition for the term data subject?

A The living individual whom the personal information is about
B Anything stored on an ICT system
C All the personal data stored about a person
D The type of personal data being stored

7 Under the Data Protection Act a data subject is allowed to see personal data held about them. If the data held about them is wrong, the data subject can do which of the following?

A   Have the right to the data being corrected or deleted

B   Have the right for the entire database to be destroyed

C   Apply for notification

D   Ring for the police

8 Which one of these statements about the Data Protection Act 1998 is false?

A   All databases have to be notified

B   You do not have to notify if you are using data for personal use

C   You do not have to notify if the data is being used for payroll

D   You may not be able to access any data held about you by the police

9 Which is the Principle designed to protect data that is held about you by an organization?

A   Data shall be fairly and lawfully processed

B   Data should be kept secure

C   Data shall be processed in accordance with data subjects' rights

D   Personal data must never be processed

10 The Electronic Communications Act 2000 is concerned with which one of these?

A   Copyright

B   Viruses

C   The use of encryption

D   Snooping

ANSWERS

Questions A

▶ **TEXTBOOK PAGE 261**

1 (a) One mark for a definition of 'personal information' and one mark for each of two examples.
   - Data about a living identifiable person that is specific to that person (1)
   - Such as medical details (1) or details about their credit history (1)

   (b) One mark for each of two points such as:
   - The information held could be wrong (1)
   - It could affect them in getting a job (1)
   - It could affect them getting credit (1)

2 (a) One mark for each of three items of personal information (NB not contact details).
   - Medical details
   - Social worker details
   - Qualifications
   - Religious beliefs
   - Etc.

   (b) One mark for each of the following:
   - The right to see the information held and have it corrected or deleted if it is wrong
   - The right to compensation if they have suffered harm because the information has been held illegally

   (c) One mark for each point/example to a maximum of two marks.
   - Their details could be mixed up with someone else (1)
   - It could affect them in getting a job (1)
   - It could stop them getting the right medical treatment if they were ill (1)

Questions B

▶ **TEXTBOOK PAGE 262**

1 One mark for The Computer Misuse Act 1990.

2 One mark for one suitable offence covered by the Act and one mark for the example. A suitable answer would be:
   - Hacking (i.e. accessing) an ICT system illegally with a view to looking at data
   - An example would be a schoolboy accessing the Ministry of Defence's computer system from their own home computer

3 Two marks, one for the name of the method and one mark for a description of the method.
   Install a firewall – this will help prevent access to the internal network from someone outside the organization such as a hacker using the Internet

4 One mark for each of two points.
   - Illegally copying software (1)
   - In breach of the licensing agreement (1)
   - Selling copies of the software to others (1)

Questions C

▶ **TEXTBOOK PAGE 264**

1 (a) One mark for the full name and date.
   Health & Safety (Display Screen Equipment) Regulations 1992

   (b) (i) One mark each for two of the following:
   - Screen should tilt and swivel
   - Screen should be at an appropriate height for the user
   - Screen should display a stable image with no flickering
   - Screen should have brightness and contrast control
   - Screen should be free from reflections (i.e., have a non-reflective coating on the screen)

   (ii) One mark each for two of the following:
   - Workstations should be big enough for computer and paperwork
   - Workstations should have a matt surface

2 (a) Any two (one mark each) from the following list:
   - Adjustable in height so that the feet can be placed flat on the floor. If this is not possible because a person is short, then a footrest should be provided
   - Have seat backs that provide proper back support (i.e., they should have adjustable height and tilt)
   - Have five feet with castors for stability and to ensure that it is easy for the chair to be moved closer to and further away from the desk

   (b) Two of the following design features (one mark each):
   - Screen should tilt and swivel
   - Screen should be at an appropriate height for the user
   - Screen should display a stable image with no flickering
   - Screen should have brightness and contrast control
   - Screen should be free from reflections (i.e., have a non-reflective coating on the screen)
   - Keep the screen clean so it is easy to make out the characters on the screen

3 (a) One mark for one of the following purposes:
   - Detect and prevent terrorism
   - Prevent and detect crime

   (b) One mark each for two ways such as:
   - Demand access to your emails, instant messages, etc., from your Internet service provider without your knowing
   - Listen in secret to phone calls and see all your text messages
   - Monitor all your searches made on the Internet

Test yourself

▶ **TEXTBOOK PAGE 265**

A Privacy
B Data Protection
C Information
D register, accurate, up-to-date
E Principles
F personal, deleted
G viruses
H hacking
I Computer Misuse
J surveillance

Examination style questions

▶ **TEXTBOOK PAGE 266**

1

	Tick if one of the Principles
Data is adequate, relevant and not excessive	√
Personal data should be adequate and kept up-to-date	√
Software should not be copied	
Personal data should only be used for one or more specified and lawful purposes	√
There must be sufficient security to cover the personal data	√
Hacking is illegal	

2 (a) One mark for a feature for the chair such as:
- Adjustable seat height
- Movable castors
- Adjustable back rest
- Five legs for stability
- Adjustable arm rests

(b) One mark for a feature for the keyboard such as:
- Tiltable
- Matt finish to reduce glare
- Area at the front to rest wrists on
- Soft pad to rest wrists on
- Ergonomic keyboard with keys arranged differently

(c) One mark for a feature for software such as:
- A font and font size used for text that is easy to see for a range of users
- Appropriate colour combinations for text and background
- Uncluttered appearance making use of drop-down menus
- Shortcuts to minimize keystrokes or mouse movements

3 (a) One mark each for three of the Data Protection Principles.
- Data should be processed fairly and lawfully
- Data should be obtained for only specified purposes
- Data should be adequate, relevant and not excessive
- Data should be accurate and kept up-to-date
- Data should be not kept any longer than is necessary
- Data should be processed in accordance with the rights of the data subject
- Data should be kept secure
- Data should not be transferred to a country outside the EU unless they have a comparable data protection law

(b) One mark for each correct answer to a maximum of two marks.

	Tick two boxes
Word-processed documents	√
Insurance company's data	
A database of friends' names and addresses	√
A database of doctors' patients	
Files stored on paper	

(c) (i) One mark for each point to a maximum of two marks:
- The person (1) whom the personal data is about (1)

(ii) One mark for each of two rights:
- The right to see the personal data and to have it corrected or deleted if it is wrong (1)
- The right to compensation if they have suffered harm due to the negligence of the organization holding the personal data (1)

4 (a) One mark for each piece of information to a maximum of three marks (NB the data must apply to a person and not to the products being ordered).
- Name
- Address
- Phone number
- Email address
- Date of birth
- Credit/debit card details

(b) One mark for an item such as:
- Credit/debit card details
- Bank account details
- Password to access account

(c) One mark for
- The data can be encrypted
- A secure site can be used

Case study 1 Cyber warfare

▶ **TEXTBOOK PAGE 267**

1 (a) One mark for each point to a maximum of three marks.
- Unauthorized access to an ICT system
- Usually but not necessarily using the Internet
- Hackers can delete important data
- This data can relate to terrorists, organized crime, etc.
- It could be medical details for the whole country
- This could easily cause loss of life
- It could cause loss of infrastructure, such as loss of air traffic control

(b) One mark for each point to a maximum of two marks.
- Firewall is hardware, software or both (1)
- Used to prevent unauthorized access to a network (1)
- Blocks requests for certain data (1)
- Looks at and examines each incoming packet of data (1)
- If packet is not of a type allowed, it is rejected (1)

2 One mark for each of two examples such as:
- Nuclear power stations
- MI5
- Central medical databases
- The Pentagon
- Armed forces computer systems
- NASA
- Etc.

3 One mark for each point to a maximum of two marks.
Agree
- Hackers have a good understanding of methods used (1)
- They can point out vulnerabilities (1)
- They know other hackers and can 'grass' on them (1)
Disagree
- Rewarding them is morally wrong (1)
- It encourages hackers as they know they will get a well-paid job (1)
- Hacking could become a career pathway (1)
- You cannot pay criminals (1)

4 One mark for The Computer Misuse Act 1990.
5 (a) One mark for each point to a maximum of two marks.
  • Encryption scrambles the data into a code (1)
  • You need a key to turn the data back to readable form (1)
  • If a hacker intercepted the data they would not be able to understand it (1)
  • If the data was stolen (e.g. on a laptop) the data would be unreadable (1)
  • Useful for sending banking details over the Internet (1)
  (b) One mark for each point to a maximum of two marks.
  • Encryption can be used by terrorists or criminals (1)
  • It enables them to have conversations in private (1)
  • Prevents surveillance from taking place (1)
  • Makes it harder for security services to collect evidence (1)
  • Harder to gain prosecutions (1)

Case study 2 Hackers destroy a flight simulation site

▶ TEXTBOOK PAGE 268

1 (a) One mark for each of two points such as:
  • A person who gains illegal access to a computer
  • A hacker can view the information or alter it
  • They usually gain access via the Internet into a supposedly secure network
  (b) One mark for The Computer Misuse Act 1990
2 (a) One mark for each of two media such as:
  • Floppy disk (unlikely though!)
  • CD/DVD
  • Portable hard drive
  • File server
  • Flash drive/pen drive
  • Memory card
  (b) One mark for answer such as:
  • In case the computer is lost
  • In case the building is destroyed with everything in it
3 One mark for each of two reasons.
  • To store a database for a network
  • To store all the files needed by a network
  • To store a website so users can access it using the Internet

Case study 3 The NHS losing patient medical records

▶ TEXTBOOK PAGE 268

1 One mark for: They could sue the NHS for negligence/harm suffered.

2 One mark for each of two Principles from the following list:
  • Data should be processed fairly and lawfully
  • Data should be obtained for only specified purposes
  • Data should be adequate, relevant and not excessive
  • Data should be not kept any longer than is necessary
  • Data should be processed in accordance with the rights of the data subject
  • Data should be kept secure
  • Data should not be transferred to a country outside the EU unless they have a comparable data protection law
3 One mark for each item (not contact details) up to three marks such as:
  • Medications taken
  • Details of tests made
  • Details of medical examinations
  • Hospital details
  • Sexuality
  • Next of kin
4 (a) One mark for each point to a maximum of two marks such as:
  • Data is scrambled/put into a code
  • You need a key to decode
  (b) One mark for:
  If someone views data, without the code they will not be able to understand it
  (c) Two ways (one mark each) such as:
  • They could be sold to insurance companies
  • They could be sold to the press if the patient was a celebrity
  • They could be blackmailed

Worksheet: Legal and ethical issues anagrams

▶ TEACHER'S RESOURCE GUIDE TOPIC 23 PAGE 156

1 Data Protection Act
2 Privacy
3 Personal data
4 Data subject
5 Hacking
6 Copyright
7 Piracy
8 Surveillance
9 Principles
10 Accurate

Multiple-choice questions

▶ TEACHER'S RESOURCE GUIDE TOPIC 23 PAGE 158

1C, 2B, 3B, 4D, 5D, 6A, 7A, 8A, 9B, 10C

▶ Worksheet 1   pp. 274–275

Staying safe online anagrams

Here are some words or phrases that have been jumbled up. The words are connected with Staying safe online. Can you work out what they are? There is a clue to help you.

1 Pearl son   *Hint: You should never reveal this type of information to a stranger.*

Answer: _____

2 Ageism   *Hint: These can be altered using editing software.*

Answer: _____

3 Repair appoint   *Hint: You should not use this type of language in chat rooms, blogs, emails, etc.*

Answer: _____

4 Nibble cry ugly   *Hint: A name for bullying using ICT such as the Internet.*

Answer: _____

5 Add remote   *Hint: Chat rooms and blogs are often _____ to check people are behaving appropriately.*

Answer: _____

6 Amen   *Hint: You should never give your real one when using chat rooms.*

Answer: _____

7 Tacts anthem   *Hint: You should not open these unless they are from people you know and trust.*

Answer: _____

8 Prenatal   *Hint: _____ controls allow parents to set controls on their children's Internet use.*

Answer: _____

9 Shy riot   *Hint: Gives the website addresses of all the recent websites visited.*

Answer: _____

10 Sealed hippo   *Hint: People who prey on young children.*

Answer: _____

Worksheet 2 — pp. 274–275

Staying safe online

Staying safe online is extremely important for everyone. Adults are usually more streetwise and wary when using online services such as chat rooms but young children can be very trusting.

You have been asked by your teacher to produce a list of dos and don'ts when using the Internet.

Dos

1 _____

_____

2 _____

_____

3 _____

_____

4 _____

_____

5 _____

_____

Don'ts

1 _____

_____

2 _____

_____

3 _____

_____

4 _____

_____

5 _____

_____

▶ Multiple-choice questions

pp. 274–275

1 Which one of the following would you *not* call personal data?

A Name
B Address
C Mobile phone number
D Sex

2 Disclosure of personal details means which one of these?

A Allowing others to tell you about themselves
B Letting others know your personal details
C Copying data
D Sending data wirelessly

3 Misuse of images would *not* mean which one of the following?

A Altering an image so that it no longer tells the truth
B Copying an image of a friend and sending it to lots of people without their permission
C Printing a photograph out
D Using an image to blackmail someone

4 A code of conduct would normally contain which one of the following?

A A list of friends
B A series of rules that you must obey
C A list of email addresses
D A list of mobile phone numbers

5 Which one of these could be an example of the misuse of an image?

A Telling a lie using an image
B Cropping an image
C Enlarging an image
D Changing an image to black and white

6 Inappropriate language should not be used in a chat room.

Which one of the following is classed as inappropriate language?

A Swearing
B Shouting
C Text language
D Programming language

7 Young children should not be allowed to use chat rooms unsupervised.

Which one of the following is the main reason for this?

A Chat rooms are only for adults
B Children do not like to chat
C People would not want to chat to children
D Paedophiles often use chat rooms to look for their next victim

8 Which one of the following should you never reveal in a chat room?

A Name
B Telephone number
C A nickname
D Age

9 **Which one of the following statements is false?**

A Chat rooms allow you to have a conversation with another person

B The person who you are chatting to is always who they say they are

C You should never reveal personal information in a chat room

D People who you chat to are strangers if you don't know them properly

10 **A young person decides to produce a website outlining some of their interests.**

Which one of the following should they never reveal on this website?

A Their age

B Their interests

C Pictures of their pets

D Their mobile phone number

ANSWERS

Questions A

▶ **TEXTBOOK PAGE 275**

1 One mark for each of two misuses. One word answers are not acceptable.
- Image sent to one person could be sent to others without the original person's permission
- Images may be altered so they no longer tell the truth
- Images could be posted onto a website without the permission of the person who supplied the images

2 (a) One mark for a network service such as:
- Social networking site
- Profile
- Chat room
- Blog

(b) One mark each for two of the following:
- You could be groomed by a paedophile
- You could be stalked
- A person you do not know might ring you
- You could have your identity stolen

Test yourself

▶ **TEXTBOOK PAGE 276**

A personal
B Paedophiles
C cyberbullying
D website
E photo editing
F Paedophiles
G inappropriate
H attachments, viruses

Examination style questions

▶ **TEXTBOOK PAGE 276**

1 (a) One mark for each facility to a maximum of two marks.
- Chat rooms
- MSN
- Social networking sites (e.g., Facebook, MySpace, Twitter, etc.)
- Blogs

(b) One mark for each relevant point to a maximum of four marks.
- People you chat to could be anyone (1)
- You may think you are chatting to a child when they are an adult (1)
- Paedophiles use these sites to meet their next victim (1)
- There have been many cases where people have been raped or murdered by people they met on the Internet (1)
- You have no way of knowing that people are genuine (1)
- The picture they sent you might not be their own (1)
- The Internet is a fantasy world to many and they tell lies on it (1)

2 (a) One mark for the example and one mark for identification of the advantage. Examples might include:
- You can find out if people you know have any friends in common with you
- You could find out if people in your road go to the same school as you
- You can find new friends that share the same interests as you

- You can contact people who are experiencing the same problems as you

(b) One mark for each point to a maximum of two marks.
- You could become a victim of identity theft
- They could find out where you live and stalk you
- You could get pestered by phone calls and emails
- They may try to tell lies about you on blogs, message boards, etc.

3 One mark for each point to a maximum of four marks. A crime might have been committed and someone tries to cover it (1) by altering a picture with a date and a time on it to show that they were somewhere else (1). They could edit the picture and put themselves in it (1). For example, it could show them at a sporting event such as a football match, which meant they could not have committed the crime (1). Could put your head on someone else's body (1) and post an embarrassing image on a social networking site (1). Paedophiles could get hold of an image of you (1) and spread the picture around other paedophiles (1).

4 One mark for each point to a maximum of four marks such as:
- Children tend to believe people and might be taken in by them (1)
- They may not be aware of the dangers (1)
- They may decide to meet someone (1)
- People you chat to could be anyone (1)
- You may think you are chatting to a child when they are an adult (1)
- Paedophiles use these sites to meet their next victim (1)
- There have been many cases where people have been raped or murdered by people they met on the Internet (1)
- You have no way of knowing that people are genuine (1)
- The picture they sent you might not be their own (1)
- The Internet is a fantasy world to many and they tell lies on it (1)

5 (a) One mark for each point/further amplification to a maximum of two marks.
- The language used might breach the code of conduct
- They may be bullying another person
- They may need to take disciplinary action

(b) One mark for an answer such as:
- They might suspend the service permanently so you cannot use it
- They might suspend the service temporarily

Worksheet 1: Staying safe online anagrams

▶ **TEACHER'S RESOURCE GUIDE TOPIC 24 PAGE 163**

1 Personal
2 Images
3 Inappropriate
4 Cyberbullying
5 Moderated
6 Name
7 Attachments
8 Parental
9 History
10 Paedophiles

Multiple-choice questions

▶ **TEACHER'S RESOURCE GUIDE TOPIC 24 PAGE 165**

1D, 2B, 3C, 4B, 5A, 6A, 7D, 8B, 9B, 10D

▶ **Case study**   p. 281

Stolen RAF data files

Unencrypted data on three hard drives was stolen from an RAF base. This data contained personal details about some senior officers in the RAF. In particular it contained details of those officers who presented more of a security risk than other officers because of their lifestyle. The data contained personal details such as which officers were in debt, which officers were drug users or were having extra-marital affairs.

The worry for the RAF was that this stolen data could be used by others to blackmail the officers concerned. They were also worried that they could be sold to journalists, who would produce articles about the senior officers concerned.

1 **(a)** Explain the meaning of the term 'unencrypted'. **(2 marks)**
  (b) Explain how the problem might not have been so serious if the data on the hard drives had been encrypted. **(2 marks)**

2 **(a)** Give the name of the law that requires organizations to take steps to keep personal information private. **(1 mark)**
  (b) It is a requirement of the Act to keep the data secure.
      Give two other requirements of the Act. **(2 marks)**

3 Describe two ways the person who stole the personal information might use it. **(2 marks)**

▶ Worksheet

Data protection issues anagrams

Here are some words or phrases that have been jumbled up. The words are connected with Data protection issues. Can you work out what they are? There is a clue to help you.

1 Prince tony   *Hint: Method of keeping data private.*

Answer: _____

2 Fair well   *Hint: Used to keep hackers out.*

Answer: _____

3 Sack her   *Hint: People who gain illegal access to a computer.*

Answer: _____

4 Cress ruin van   *Hint: Software used to scan for viruses.*

Answer: _____

5 Manic fun lot   *Hint: Problem with equipment not working.*

Answer: _____

6 Buck pa   *Hint: You must remember to take this.*

Answer: _____

7 Cattleman thief   *Hint: Can be sent with an email.*

Answer: _____

8 Beetle raid   *Hint: Not by accident.*

Answer: _____

9 Cress lamb   *Hint: What encryption does to the data.*

Answer: _____

10 Error sure   *Hint: Mistake made by the user.*

Answer: _____

▶ Activity 1 p. 281

The trouble caused by viruses

Viruses cause computer users all sorts of problems and you may have had problems with them yourself. Viruses can cause organizations huge amounts of problems that cost a lot of money to put right.

For this activity you have to use the Internet to find some examples of the problems caused by virus attacks.

Collect your research material and then produce a word-processed document that outlines four cases where viruses have caused problems.

▶ Activity 2   pp. 280–281

Keeping viruses out

There are many ways you can keep viruses out of an ICT system.

You have to produce a poster for the computer room outlining what steps a user can take to keep viruses out of their system.

▶ Multiple-choice questions

pp. 280–281

1 Unauthorized access to a computer system is called which one of these?

A Data protection
B Phishing
C Worm
D Hacking

2 Which one of the following statements about firewalls is false?

A Firewalls prevent communication that is not allowed between two networks
B Firewalls can be software
C Firewalls can be hardware
D Firewalls can encourage the spreading of viruses

3 Which one of the following best describes the purpose of a firewall?

A It is used to protect a high security network when connected to a low security network such as the Internet
B It is used to connect a computer to the Internet
C It is used to enable several computers in a network to gain access to the Internet
D It is used to stop viruses spreading around an internal network

4 Threats to an ICT system may be human or non-human in origin.

Which one of the following is non-human in origin?

A Earthquakes
B Viruses
C User errors
D Hackers

5 Which one of the following is *not* a method of preventing unauthorized access to a computer?

A Keyboard locks
B Swipe cards
C Disk drive locks
D Lists of passwords

6 A user who wants to gain access to an ICT system needs to enter a password first. Most systems only allow you to try a password a few times before it locks you out of the system completely. Which one of these is the correct reason for this?

A It may be someone unauthorized trying to enter different passwords to hack into the system
B The password needs to be entered several times before it will work
C To prevent viruses entering the system
D To cause annoyance to the user

7 Which of the following is *not* a threat to an ICT system?

A Hacking
B Viruses
C Fire
D Updates

8 Abuse of computers by staff can be accidental or deliberate?

Which one of the following could *not* be accidental?

A Damage caused by dropping a laptop computer
B Erasing data
C Copying data and passing it to a competitor
D Introducing a virus

pp. 280–281

▶ Multiple-choice questions
(continued)

9 Encryption works by which one of these?

A Coding and decoding data
B Sending the password as an email
C Asking for the data to be kept secret
D By signing the Official Secrets Act

10 Some of the latest systems software encrypts the data when it is stored on the hard drive. Why is this done?

A So that more data can be stored on the hard drive
B It is easier for the computer to store encrypted data
C Encrypted data cannot be read without the key
D So that the data is stored more accurately

ANSWERS

Questions A

▶ **TEXTBOOK PAGE 281**

1 (a) One mark for each method × 2.
- Accidental erasure of files
- Bugs in software causing damage to files
- Equipment malfunction
- Dropping equipment

(b) One mark for each method × 2.
- Deliberate destruction of data and programs by own staff
- Damage caused by hackers
- Virus attack causing loss of data
- Theft of equipment

2 One mark for each point or example to a maximum of four marks.
- Data takes time and effort to build up (1). For example, a large customer database could take years to create (1)
- Data is almost impossible to re-create if original data is lost and no backups have been taken (1). An example would be a firm going out of business after losing all its data (1)
- Data is commercially valuable (1), as competitors to a business would love to have a copy of the data (1)
- Data is very expensive to create, as resources need to be used to create it (1). For example, you may have to pay people to type the data in (1)

Test yourself

▶ **TEXTBOOK PAGE 282**

A Training
B accidental
C tested
D firewall
E scanner
F file attachments
G download
H passwords

Examination style questions

▶ **TEXTBOOK PAGE 282**

1 (a) One mark each for two threats:
- Install smoke detectors
- Install a sprinkler system
- Keep backup copies of software and data in fireproof safe
- Keep backup copies off-site
- Do not keep large quantities of combustible material, such as paper, in the computer room

(b) One mark each for two threats:
- Keep notes of all serial numbers of computers – more chance of getting them back
- Encrypt data stored on hard drives, so others cannot see the data stored
- Keep backup copies of all the hard drives
- Physically attach computers to the desks using cables
- Only allow entry by authorized staff to rooms containing computers

(c) One mark each for two threats:
- Use firewalls to prevent theft of data by hackers
- Do not allow staff to use removable media

- Do not allow data to be copied onto removable media (or copied without permission)
- Use locks that prevent removable media being inserted

2 (a) One mark for each threat, which must be due to the Internet x3.
- Virus attack
- Hackers accessing data
- Identity theft

(b) One mark for answer which must apply to one of the answers in part (a).
- Virus attack – opening file attachments from people you don't know will increase the threat of virus attack
- Hackers accessing data – install a firewall that will prevent people accessing the internal network from the Internet
- Identity theft – install virus checkers that check for programs that can store passwords and usernames and transmit them to a fraudster using the Internet

3 (a) Two items (one mark each) from the following list:
- Credit card numbers
- Money transfers using Internet banks from one account to another
- Personal details when applying for loans
- Online transactions between companies
- Data in emails

(b) Two marks for explanation of encryption and an example or more amplification.
- The process of coding data, sending it over the Internet and then deciphering it when it reaches the true recipient, is called encryption. Credit card numbers are encrypted when sent over the Internet so that they cannot be used by hackers
- Data is sometimes encrypted when saved onto portable media such as a portable hard drive or flash drive. This is in case it is stolen, the thief will be unable to read or understand the information stored

4 (a) One mark for one reason such as:
- A username is a name used to identify a particular user to the network
- So that they can be allocated network resources such as storage area, access to certain programs and data files

(b) One mark for one reason such as:
- A password is used to restrict access to ICT systems to only those people allowed access. It involves a user typing in a series of characters that only they should know

(c) One mark each for three such as:
- Use a combination of upper and lower case characters
- Use numbers and other non-alphabetic characters in the password
- Do not use words or names for passwords

Case study: Stolen RAF data files

▶ **TEACHER'S RESOURCE GUIDE TOPIC 25 PAGE 168**

1 (a) One mark for each point to a maximum of two marks.
- Data which has not been scrambled (1)
- And can be intercepted and read by hackers (1)

- Or viewed by others if the computer/media the files are on is lost or stolen (1)
(b) One mark for each point to a maximum of two marks.
  - Only the person with the key to the code is able to read it (1)
  - The data would all be jumbled up/scrambled (1)
  - If someone steals the computer or media then the data will be meaningless (1)

2 (a) One mark for The Data Protection Act 1998.
  (b) One mark each for two of the Data Protection Principles:
  Personal data should be:
  1. processed fairly and lawfully
  2. obtained for only specified purposes
  3. adequate, relevant and not excessive
  4. accurate and kept up-to-date
  5. not kept any longer than is necessary
  6. processed in accordance with the rights of the data subject
  7. not transferred to a country unless they have a comparable data protection law

3 One mark each for two of the following:
  - Can be used to commit fraud
  - Can be used to blackmail someone
  - Can be used to commit identity theft

Worksheet: Data protection issues anagrams
▶ **TEACHER'S RESOURCE GUIDE TOPIC 25 PAGE 169**

1 Encryption
2 Firewall
3 Hackers
4 Virus scanners
5 Malfunction
6 Backup
7 File attachment
8 Deliberate
9 Scrambles
10 User error

Multiple-choice questions
TEACHER'S RESOURCE GUIDE TOPIC 25 PAGE 172

1D, 2D, 3A, 4A, 5D, 6A, 7D, 8C, 9A, 10C

▶ Worksheet   pp. 286–287

Health issues anagrams

Here are some words or phrases that have been jumbled up. The words are connected with Health issues. Can you work out what they are? There is a clue to help you.

1 A retentive injury trip is   *Hint: RSI.*

Answer: _____

2 Erase tiny   *Hint: You get this by looking at the screen for long periods.*

Answer: _____

3 A cab heck   *Hint: Incorrect posture when sitting gives you this.*

Answer: _____

4 Chase head   *Hint: Eye strain can give you these.*

Answer: _____

5 Jab saluted   *Hint: All chairs used with computers should be this.*

Answer: _____

6 Cut demon   *Hint: A _____ holder.*

Answer: _____

7 Large   *Hint: Use blinds on windows to prevent this on the screen.*

Answer: _____

8 Crime goons   *Hint: The science of making thing used by humans easier to use.*

Answer: _____

9 Pouters   *Hint: Incorrect _____ can cause back ache.*

Answer: _____

10 Burr led   *Hint: Stress and headaches can give rise to this problem with vision.*

Answer: _____

▶ Activity 1 | pp. 286–287

Creating an interactive presentation on health and safety issues at work

Every new employee of an organization gets an induction pack when they start work at the organization. Part of this induction pack consists of some health and safety training on the safe use of ICT equipment.

You have been asked to produce a presentation using presentation software.

There are a number of requirements of the system and these are:
- The system is intended to be used by one employee at a time sitting at a computer.
- The system must be easy to use, as they will be working on their own.
- It should be possible for the user to decide what they want to do next, so you will need some form of navigation around the system.
- The presentation should be fun to use.
- The target audience will be employees, so your presentation must meet their needs.
- Appropriate images should be included.
- You could try including some health and safety video if you can find a source.

▶ Activity 2 | pp. 286–287

Researching equipment that will reduce the risk of potential health hazards when working with ICT

There are many pieces of equipment that can be used to reduce the risk of potential health hazards when working with ICT.

In this activity you have to research them.

For each piece of equipment you need to obtain an image and write a few sentences about its purpose and what potential health hazard it avoids.

▶ Activity 3 | pp. 286–287

What are these for?

Here are some health and safety products that can be used to help prevent certain health problems when staff use computers. Can you identify them and work out what each of them is for? Write a short sentence to explain.

1

Answer: _____

2

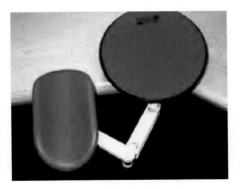

Answer: _____

3

Answer: _____

Activity 3
(continued)

pp. 286–287

4

Answer: _____

5

Answer: _____

6

Answer: _____

7

Answer: _____

▶ Multiple-choice questions

pp. 286–287

1 Which one of these medical complaints is not usually caused by using computers?

A Eye strain
B Repetitive strain injury
C Back ache
D A sprained ankle

2 There is a law that lays down minimum standards for computer systems and furniture. Which one of these is *not* a requirement of this law?

A Adjustable chairs
B No reflections off the screen
C Plenty of pot plants
D Display screens that do not flicker

3 RSI is the name of an injury that may be caused by the incorrect use of keyboards. What does RSI stand for?

A Repetitive strain injury
B Resultant sitting infirmity
C Relatively stable interface
D Repetitive sprain injury

4 People who look at a computer screen for long periods of time may experience eye strain. Which one of the following is not a way of preventing eye strain?

A Use a copyholder
B Have frequent eye-tests
C Use suitable lighting
D Make sure that an adjustable chair is used

5 To avoid RSI a computer user should do which one of the following?

A Use a keyboard as much as they can
B Use a mouse as much as they can
C Use a wrist rest when typing or using a mouse
D Use a copyholder

6 Eye strain is a problem which can cause blurred vision and headaches.

Which one of the following would *not* help a user prevent eye strain?

A Take regular breaks
B Keep the screen clean
C Use appropriate lighting and blinds to avoid glare
D Use a wrist rest

7 Working with ICT systems can be very stressful.

Which one of the following situations is *not* stressful?

A Using badly designed software
B Using a graphical user interface
C Losing work due to a virus attack
D Trying to meet unreasonable deadlines

8 A business owner is looking at computer screens to check that they meet the current health and safety requirements.

Which of the following is *not* one of the requirements for screens?

A Computer screens should be capable of tilt and swivel
B The screen should be free from reflections
C It must be of an appropriate size for the software application being used
D The screen must be in colour

▶ **Multiple-choice questions**
(continued)

pp. 286–287

9 **Which of the following is *not* a requirement for a chair used by a computer user in a business?**

A It should have an adjustable backrest
B The seat height should be adjustable
C The base should have five points and castors
D The chair should be made of fabric

10 **Back ache can be caused by which one of the following?**

A Incorrect posture
B Badly designed software
C Operating systems
D Touch screens

ANSWERS

Questions A

▶ **TEXTBOOK PAGE 286**

1 (a) One mark for 'repetitive strain injury'.
   (b) One mark for symptoms (e.g., painful joints, swelling of hands/fingers).
        One mark for the cause (e.g., typing at high speed, using a keyboard, using a mouse, using a games joystick/controller, etc.).

2 (a) Two health problems, one mark each, such as:
        • Repetitive strain injury (RSI)
        • Back ache
        • Stress
        • Eye strain
        • Obesity or other illnesses related to inactivity
   (b) One mark for:
        • Losing work
        • Virus attack
        • Not being able to access the Internet
        • Problems with hardware
        • Too much work to do in too little time
        • Having to learn new software/hardware
        • Technical problems

Questions B

▶ **TEXTBOOK PAGE 288**

1 (a) One mark for each of three health problems (no mark for a one word answer) such as:
        • Back ache caused by incorrect posture when sitting in a chair
        • Repetitive strain injury (RSI) caused by typing at high speed
        • Eye strain caused by focusing on the screen for too long
        • Stress caused by computer problems, bad software design, etc.
   (b) One mark for each of six points such as:
        • Use an adjustable chair (NB in work this is a legal requirement but you need to ensure that the chair you use at home is adjustable)
        • Always check the adjustment of the chair to make sure it is suitable for your height. Use a foot support called a footrest if necessary
        • Sit up straight on the chair with your feet flat on the floor
        • Make sure the screen is lined up and tilted at an appropriate angle
        • Use appropriate lighting and blinds to avoid glare, which can cause headaches
        • Take regular breaks to avoid stress and give your eyes a rest
        • Have regular eye-tests (NB if you use a screen in your work, then your employer is required by law to pay for regular eye-tests and glasses if they are needed for work)
        • Ensure you are not sitting too near the screen, to avoid the possible risks of radiation
        • Keep the screen clean so it is easy to make out the characters on the screen

2 (a) One mark for repetitive strain injury.
   (b) One mark for one of the following:
        • Aches and pain in hands
        • Aches and pains in wrists
        • Aches and pains in arms
        • Aches and pains in neck
   (c) One mark each for two of the following precautions:
        • Adjust your chair to the correct seating position for you
        • Make sure there is enough space to work comfortably
        • Use a document holder
        • Use a wrist rest
        • Keep your wrists straight when keying in
        • Position the mouse so that it can be used keeping the wrist straight
        • Learn how to type properly – two finger typing has been found to be much worse for RSI

3 One mark for each tick placed in the correct column.

	True	False
The continual use of keyboards over a long period can give rise to aches and pains in the hands, arms and wrists	√	
RSI stands for repeated stress injury		√
Wrist rests and ergonomic keyboards can help prevent RSI	√	
Back ache can be caused by slouching in your chair when using a computer	√	
Glare on the screen can cause RSI		√

Test yourself

▶ **TEXTBOOK PAGE 289**

A Repetitive strain injury
B eye strain
C headaches
D back ache
E back ache
F eye strain
G blinds
H eye-tests
I Stress
J Stress
K easy

Examination style questions

▶ **TEXTBOOK PAGE 290**

1 (a) One mark for repetitive strain injury.
   (b) One mark for each point to a maximum of two marks.
        • Caused by typing at high speed (1) or using a mouse over a long period of time (1)
        • Caused by working in cramped conditions (1)
        • Caused by repeatedly moving head a certain way to read a document and look at the screen (1)
   (c) One mark for one of the following:
        • Adjust your chair to the correct seating position for you
        • Make sure there is enough space to work comfortably
        • Use a document holder
        • Use an ergonomic keyboard/mouse
        • Use a wrist rest
        • Keep your wrists straight when keying in
        • Position the mouse so that it can be used keeping the wrist straight
        • Learn how to type properly – two finger typing has been found to be much worse for RSI

2 One mark each for:
- Back ache
- Stress
- Repetitive strain injury (RSI)
- Eye strain

3 (a) One mark for each of two health problems (not eye strain or RSI) such as:
- Back ache
- Neck ache
- Stress
- Headaches

(b) One mark each for two methods of prevention.
- Back ache – use an adjustable chair and make sure you adjust it to suit your height; you can use a foot rest if there is one
- Neck ache – ensure the screen is positioned in front of the user/ensure a copyholder is used
- Stress – make sure that users get good training so they are not stressed by the changes they have to cope with
- Headaches – make sure that fluorescent tubes are used with diffusers on them to spread out the light

Worksheet: Health issues anagrams

▶ **TEACHER'S RESOURCE GUIDE TOPIC 26 PAGE 176**

1 Repetitive strain injury
2 Eye strain
3 Back ache
4 Headaches

5 Adjustable
6 Document
7 Glare
8 Ergonomics
9 Posture
10 Blurred

Activity 3: What are these for?

▶ **TEACHER'S RESOURCE GUIDE TOPIC 26 PAGE 179**

1 Mouse mat with a wrist rest filled with gel so that a user is less likely to suffer with RSI.
2 An adjustable arm rest with a mouse mat – used to reduce the likelihood of RSI occurring when using a mouse.
3 A wrist rest to be placed at the front of the keyboard. Provides a cushion for when a user is typing at high speed – it reduces the likelihood of RSI.
4 A foot rest to help a user (particularly a short user) adopt the correct posture when working at a computer.
5 An anti-glare or anti-radiation filter. Used to cut down glare, which could cause eye strain and/or headaches. Could also reduce the risk of radiation from the screen, although this is very debatable.
6 An ergonomic mouse – could reduce the likelihood of RSI.
7 A foot-controlled mouse – may reduce likelihood of RSI.

Multiple-choice questions

▶ **TEACHER'S RESOURCE GUIDE TOPIC 26 PAGE 181**

1D, 2C, 3A, 4D, 5C, 6D, 7B, 8D, 9D, 10A

▶ Case study 1 `pp. 296–297`

Wikipedia

Wikipedia was set up to empower and engage people around the world by collecting and offering free content that can be disseminated globally. It is a huge success story and has changed the way the Internet is used.

You will probably have already used Wikipedia but if not take a look at it now at: www.wikipedia.com.

Wikipedia is a charity and unlike most other free providers of content, it does not contain adverts and therefore gets no money from these sources. Instead it relies mainly on asking you and me to donate money, or on revenue from grants. The money it obtains is used to buy hardware and also for hosting and bandwidth costs. People are not paid to add content – they do it for free!

Wikipedia is best described as an online encyclopaedia but it is different from other encyclopaedias in so much as it is made up from contributions by ordinary people. You may think this is a bad thing. After all, what if the information is wrong? It is easy to put in bogus information or information that someone believes is true but isn't. Luckily, other people can add information that corrects the information that is already there. The idea is that if enough people contribute, then the information is as good as that provided more traditionally.

1 One commenter on Wikipedia said, 'There is plenty of bogus information on the Internet. What we don't want is non-experts making any old rubbish up on Wikipedia and then our children getting hold of it and believing it to be true.'

   Give a reason why this is less likely to happen than the commenter thinks. **(2 marks)**

2 You have been asked to give a brief description of what Wikipedia is to someone who has little knowledge of ICT.
   Describe Wikipedia in easy to understand non-technical language. You should make at least **three** main points in your description. **(3 marks)**

3 Wikipedia mainly consists of webpages containing text and images with links to other webpages.
   Describe **three** future developments to Wikipedia that you could reasonably foresee that would improve it. **(3 marks)**

▶ Case study 2 | pp. 296–297

A novel use for nanotechnology

The SmartShirt system uses a shirt that monitors an individual's heart rate, respiration and movement wirelessly and remotely. The shirt consists of a patented nanotechnology conductive fibre grid that is knitted into the material of the shirt. The shirt works by collecting signals from the wearer's body and then digitizing them and sending them wirelessly to a base station. A computer can then be used to decide whether action should be taken on the basis of the readings it receives.

Potential uses of this technology include:
- Monitoring patients who have just had operations.
- Monitoring elderly people living at home.
- Monitoring babies whose parents are worried about cot death.
- Monitoring truckers or other long distance drivers.
- Training for athletes.

One doctor spoke of the advantages of the system saying, 'This shirt system gives health care professionals early warning of abnormalities and access to the data they need to make smart decisions for their patients. These vital functions can be measured even if their patients are miles away.'

1 (a) Explain what is meant by the term 'nanotechnology'. **(2 marks)**

  (b) Explain how the use of nanotechnology works with the SmartShirt system outlined in the case study. **(3 marks)**

  (c) Describe **two** benefits that this system offers to society. **(2 marks)**

2 The rapid development of technologies such as the Internet and nanotechnology gives rise to a number of problems.

  Outline **one** problem caused by the use of nanotechnology. **(2 marks)**

3 Sensors have been available for years and it has also been possible to send data wirelessly from sensors. Describe **one** advantage that the SmartShirt system offers compared to the use of sensors. **(2 marks)**

▶ Case study 3 | pp. 296–297

Virtual visitor

Irobot® ConnectR is a new kind of connection device that can be used by busy parents and distant grandparents seeking greater connection and involvement with their children, grandchildren and pets.

By combining Internet connectivity and robotics the device lets you remotely visit loved ones, relatives and pets from anywhere. You can hear, see and interact with them just as if you were there in person.

You can move the robot remotely around the home of the person you wish to communicate with by using a keyboard or joystick or a special remote control. You can see around the host's house using the web camera on the robot. Speakers and microphones can be used to communicate with the host.

The Irobot® ConnectR enables remote communication.

The web camera can be controlled remotely so you can zoom in and out.

Case study 3
(continued)

pp. 296–297

The robot can be controlled remotely using the easy to use HCI (human–computer interface). It can be moved around in any direction thus enabling the user to see, hear and interact with whomever you want.

In case the host wants privacy, they can turn off the audio, video or both.

1   The virtual visitor has a number of applications.

  (a) Explain how remote working has enabled this device to be produced. **(2 marks)**

  (b) Describe two different applications for the Irobot® ConnectR. **(2 marks)**

2   Discuss the privacy issues in using the Irobot® ConnectR. **(2 marks)**

▶ **Worksheet** pp. 296–297

Researching emerging technologies

Emerging technologies change the way ICT will be used in the future. New technologies are being discovered and developed all the time.

You are required to do your own research using the Internet and write a short paragraph under each of the following headings. You also need to include the URLs (i.e. website addresses) of any websites you used to find the information.

1   Touch screen interfaces

Websites used:

_____

_____

_____

Description:

_____

_____

_____

_____

_____

_____

2   Voice recognition systems

Websites used:

_____

_____

_____

Description:

_____

_____

_____

▶ Worksheet
(continued)

pp. 296–297

_____
_____
_____

3 New uses for mobile phones

Websites used:

_____
_____
_____

Description:

_____
_____
_____
_____
_____
_____

4 The use of robots in the home

Websites used:

_____
_____
_____

Description:

_____
_____
_____
_____
_____

▶ Activity
pp. 296–297

Emerging technologies

In ICT you have to keep up with the latest technology.

Here are a number of websites that keep you up-to-date.

Look at these sites and collect some research material that you can refer to when you revise for your examination.

The following website looks at emerging technologies for learning:

http://emergingtechnologies.becta.org.uk/

The following website looks at emerging technologies in businesses:

http://news.zdnet.co.uk/emergingtech/

The following website looks at emerging technologies in the home:

http://www.masshightech.com/stories/2008/07/28/focus4-The-future-home-offers-efficiency,-entertainment-and-advice.html

▶ Multiple-choice questions   pp. 296–297

1 Some schools are starting to use biometric devices for the purpose of registering students. Which one of these is *not* a biometric method used in schools?

A   Fingerprinting
B   Retinal scanning
C   Face recognition
D   DNA

2 Flexible computer screens are likely to bring huge advantages to society.

Which one of the following is *not* one of these advantages?

A   Updatable newspapers that can be folded out
B   Large folding screens for presentations
C   Portable DVD players with a large screen
D   Smaller keyboards

3 Which one of the following is *not* a reason for the widespread use of ICT?

A   Lower cost of ICT hardware
B   Cheap communication methods such as access to the Internet
C   The increase in ICT legislation
D   The development of email and file transfer

4 Which one of the following best describes Wikipedia?

A   It is a comprehensive paper-based encyclopaedia
B   It is an online encyclopaedia with contributions by world experts
C   An encyclopaedia on CD-ROM
D   An online encyclopaedia with contributions from ordinary people

5 Which one of the following devices is *not* a mobile communication device?

A   A mobile phone
B   A PDA
C   A laptop computer
D   A desktop computer

6 Which one of the following statements concerning Bluetooth is correct?

A   Bluetooth is a standard for sending data wirelessly between devices
B   Using Bluetooth you can only transfer data using wires
C   Bluetooth technology is never used in mobile phones
D   Bluetooth is a type of computer virus

7 Which one of the following is *not* a benefit to society in the increased use of robotics?

A   Goods are made to a higher standard which means they are more reliable
B   Robots enable goods to be produced at lower cost
C   In the near future you will start to see robots being used in the home
D   Robots can only ever carry out one type of task

8 Which one of the following is not a benefit to society in using ICT?

A   Greater democracy with the use of e-voting
B   Improvement in health and life expectancy owing to advances in scanner technology
C   More flexible working makes it easier for people to fit work around family
D   Greater abuse of ICT systems

pp. 296–297

▶ Multiple-choice questions
(continued)

9 There are a number of things that limit the use of ICT.

Which one of the following is *not* one of them?

A Speed of transfer of data through communication channels

B Storage capacity

C The ability of people to learn new things

D Battery life

10 There are many legal issues caused by the development of ICT systems.

Which one of the following would *not* be expected to give rise to legal implications?

A Biometric input methods such as fingerprinting and retinal scanning

B The use of ICT for the input of names and addresses for mail shots

C Using someone else's wireless connection to gain access to the Internet without them knowing or giving permission

D Posting lies about a person on a blog or message board

ANSWERS

Questions A

▶ **TEXTBOOK PAGE 298**

1 (a) One mark for the name of the device and one mark for each additional point to a maximum of three marks. Example answers include:

Email
- You do not have to waste time printing the letter, putting it into an envelope and posting it (1)
- If the person is sitting at their desk and their computer is switched on then the email will arrive almost instantly (1)
- It is possible to send an email to lots of different people. With a letter this would be time consuming (1)
- It costs little money to send an email (1)

The Internet
- Many more people now spend their time surfing the Internet rather than watching television (1)
- You can use the Internet for playing games, watching TV programmes, listening to radio, downloading music, etc.
- The Internet has changed the way people shop, as many people now shop online
- People benefit from the lower costs of Internet goods, and shops have to lower prices to remain competitive

(b) One mark for the name or brief description of the emerging technology and one mark for a description of why it is likely to change society. Examples include:
- Smart cars – reduce traffic accidents as developments in computer control make it much harder to crash a car (1). Sensors and computers work out distances between vehicles, and brakes are applied automatically when distances become too close (1)
- Flexible screens – these allow devices to have much larger screens yet keep the device as small as possible (1). It will be possible to have moving images in books and magazines (1)

2 (a) Note that as this is a 'discuss' question, the answers should be given in continuous prose and not as a series of bulleted points.
One mark for each point to a maximum of six such as:
- High speed wireless Internet access – means you can stream video, watch movies on planes, etc.
- Low power computer chips – means that battery life is extended
- High capacity storage – lots of files can be stored in a very small space
- Touch screen technology – allows users to use the screen to enter data, eliminating the need for a very small keyboard that is difficult to use
- File compression utilities – allows large files to be attached to emails and sent over the Internet quickly
- Different file compression formats – allow the storage of lots of music tracks or digital photographs on portable media
- The use of LCD screens for making laptops small and light
- Use of interfaces that make the devices as easy to use as possible
- Combining more than one device – some mobile phones have sat nav facility and most are MP3 players

(b) One mark each for two limitations such as:
- Weight – many mobile devices are still heavy owing to heavy batteries, transformers, hard drives, etc.
- Size – if device is kept small then it makes the user interface harder to use, as any keyboard has keys that are very small
- Battery life – mobile devices can only be used away from the mains power for a limited amount of time. This limits their use on long journeys without carrying backup battery supplies

Test yourself

▶ **TEXTBOOK PAGE 299**

A packaging
B welding, paint
C vacuuming, mowing
D Nanotechnology
E storage
F voice
G accidents
H mobile

Examination style questions

▶ **TEXTBOOK PAGE 299**

1 One mark for each example to a maximum of two marks.
- Paint sprays
- Assembly of components
- Packing boxes
- Welding panels in a car factory
- Bomb disposal
- Lawn mowing
- Cleaning the floor/vacuuming

2 One mark for the example and one mark for the reason why suited.
- Mowing a lawn (1) because the task is repetitive and can be shown to the robot beforehand (1). Limited intelligence is needed for the task (1)
- Vacuum cleaning a floor (1). The cleaner only needs to work out where it has been and to avoid obstacles (1)

3 One mark for each point to a maximum of three marks.
- Use of high speed wireless broadband links
- Better batteries that hold their charge for longer
- Processors that use less power
- Lighter components
- Use of touch screen technology
- Use of voice recognition technology
- Use of LCD displays

Case study 1: Wikipedia

▶ **TEACHER'S RESOURCE GUIDE TOPIC 27 PAGE 185**

1 Two points (one mark each) such as:
- Most people would not waste their time posting incorrect information (1)
- The many users would spot the incorrect information and have it corrected (1)
- Users can use the older information that will have been edited and is less likely to misinform (1)

2 Three points (one mark each) such as:
- An encyclopaedia written collaboratively by volunteers (1)
- Anyone with access to the Internet can edit it (1)
- Anyone can add new material, references or citations (1)
- Older articles tend to be more balanced because they are edited more (1)

3 One mark for each point to a maximum of three marks. Do not worry too much if the development already exists, as long as it is not something like the ability to search text, print sections of text, etc.
- Audio – that would read out the text, which would be useful for people with impaired eyesight (1)
- Use of video – showing videos that are connected with the text and can help explain it (1)
- Use of animations – to explain how things work (1)

Case study 2: A novel use for nanotechnology

TEACHER'S RESOURCE GUIDE TOPIC 27 PAGE 186

1 (a) An explanation similar to the following for two marks:
- The science of new materials where standard sized particles can be reduced to sizes as small as a nanometre (1) where the material starts to experience strange but useful properties (1)
- New materials that exhibit strange properties because of their size (1) and are likely to have many uses in ICT such as flexible display technologies and e-paper (1)

(b) Three distinctly different points (one mark each).
- A wire grid of nanotechnology fibres is knitted into the material of the shirt (1)
- These fibres collect signals from the wearer's body and digitize them and send them wirelessly to a base station (1)
- The computer can then decide what to do based on the data it receives (1)

(c) One mark for each benefit to a maximum of two such as:
- The shirt can be used to monitor patients who have just had operations (1)

- Shirts can be used to monitor the performance of athletes (1)

2 Any suitable problem with two points for two marks such as:
- Those technologically advanced countries will be able to benefit by the development (1), which will once again widen the gap between the 'haves' and the 'have nots'
- People are not aware of the dangers of some of these materials (1) and there is a danger that some of these materials could enter humans and cause damage (1)

3 One mark for the statement of the advantage and one mark for further detail.
The shirt just looks like an ordinary tee shirt so it does not make the wearer self-conscious (1) as there are no trailing wires and large data loggers (1)

Case study 3: Virtual visitor

▶ **TEACHER'S RESOURCE GUIDE TOPIC 27 PAGE 187**

1 (a) One mark for each answer to a maximum of two marks.
- By the use of the Internet (1)
- and with wireless connectivity to the robot device (1)
- that allows the device to be controlled using a distant computer (1)

(b) Two applications (one mark each) such as:
- Being able to communicate with pets you have to leave in the house all day while you are at work (1)
- Being able to check that elderly relatives are OK and to chat with them (1)

2 Two points (one mark each) such as:
- This device could be used to spy on someone without their knowledge (1)
- The manufacturers have addressed some of the issues by enabling the person who has the Irobot in their home to turn off the audio, video or both (1)

Multiple-choice questions

▶ **TEACHER'S RESOURCE GUIDE TOPIC 27 PAGE 192**

1D, 2D, 3C, 4D, 5D, 6A, 7D, 8D, 9C, 10B

Acknowledgements

Folens Limited would like to thank the following for giving permission to use copyright material.

Teacher's Resource Guide

The author and publisher would like to thank the following for permission to reproduce copyright material:

pp. 90–93, © These images are copyright of Vanessa/Fotolia, © WebButtonsInc, © JJava; p. 142, © 36clicks; p. 170, © V. Yakobchuk; p. 179 and p. 180, © The Office Safety Company and © Fentek Industries; p. 187 and p. 188, iRobot.

Microsoft product screenshots reprinted with permission from Microsoft Corporation.

PowerPoint presentations

Topic 1, © Ziggy Smolinski/Fotolia; © Christos Georghiou/Fotolia; © Roman Milert/Fotolia; © Maria.P/Fotolia; © Dušan Zidar/Fotolia; © Joanna Zielinska/Fotolia; **Topic 2,** © Chris/Fotolia; © Imagery Majestic/Fotolia; © IKO/Fotolia; © Jaimie Duplass/Fotolia; © Jose Manuel Gelpi/Fotolia; © helix/Fotolia; **Topic 3,** © titimel35/Fotolia; © patrimonio design Fotolia; © amorphis/Fotolia; © Phototom/Fotolia; © Gilles PARNALLAND/Fotolia; **Topic 4,** GreenGate; © treenabeena/Fotolia; **Topic 5,** DRS Data Services Ltd; © Speedfighter/Fotolia; © Graça Victoria/Fotolia; © Kirill Roslyakov/Fotolia; © Michelle D. Parker/Fotolia; **Topic 12,** © morganimation/Fotolia; © julien tromeur/Fotolia; © treenabeena/Fotolia; © Marc Dietrich/Fotolia; © treenabeena/Fotolia; © Vanessa/Fotolia; © JJAVA/Fotolia; © treenabeena/Fotolia; © puentes/Fotolia; © Arto/Fotolia; © christemo/Fotolia; **Topic 15,** © Andres Rodrigo Gonzalez Buzzio/Fotolia; © Marc Dietrich/Fotolia; © Labrador/Fotolia; © Glenn Jenkinson/Fotolia; © Cyril Comtat/Fotolia; © Andres Rodriguez/Fotolia; Steve Doyle; © almagami/Fotolia **Topic 18,** © Marlee/Fotolia; © Renewer/Fotolia; © James Steidl/Fotolia; © Graça Victoria/Fotolia; © ktsdesign/Fotolia; © Anthony Hall/Fotolia; © U.P.images/Fotolia; © sint/Fotolia; © NatUlrich/Fotolia; © streetphotoru/Fotolia; **Topic 19,** © Francesco Bisignani/Fotolia; © Marc Dietrich/Fotolia; © Lotfi M./Fotolia/Fotolia; © Tan Kian Khoon/Fotolia; © Andrzej Tokarski/Fotolia; © Sergey Ivanov /Fotolia; © Stephen Coburn/Fotolia; © Georgios Alexandris/Fotolia; © Akhilesh Sharma/Fotolia; **Topic 20,** © Kyle Smith/Fotolia; © TimC/Fotolia; © The Blowfish/Fotolia Inc; © Iosif Szasz-Fabian/Fotolia; **Topic 21,** © Alister Jupp/Fotolia; © Maria.P./Fotolia; © ekzman/Fotolia; © Monkey Business Images/Shutterstock **Topic 22,** © Brian Jackson/Fotolia; © Alexey Popov/Fotolia; © Stephen Finn/Fotolia; © juanjo tugores/Fotolia; © Feng Yu/Fotolia; © Eisenhans/Fotolia; © kentoh/Fotolia; **Topic 24,** © Alexey Klementiev/Fotolia; © iQoncept/Fotolia; © godfer/Fotolia; **Topic 25,** © Pixel/Fotolia; © Yong Hian Lim/Fotolia; © Helder Almeida/Fotolia; © Kirill R/Shutterstock; © doug Olson/Fotolia; © isyste/Fotolia; **Topic 26,** © bilderbox/Fotolia; © Adam Borkowski/Fotolia; © doug Olson/Fotolia; © amaxim/Fotolia; © ikon-spiracy/Fotolia; © Dmitry Nikolaev/Fotolia; ds-ergonomics; **Topic 27,** © Yakov Stavchansky/Fotolia; © Daniel Bujack/Fotolia

Microsoft product screenshots reprinted with permission from Microsoft Corporation.

Every effort has been made to contact copyright holders of material used in this publication. If any copyright holder has been overlooked, we should be pleased to make any necessary arrangements.